W9-CQI-611

My First
Atlas
Discovering Our World

General Director: Philippe Auzou
Senior Editor: Gwenaëlle Hamon
English Version Editor: Nel Yomtov
Texts: Sabrina Lanneluc, Marie-France Delhomme
(school teacher) and Audrey Privat-Colnat for l'AS DES COURS (formation and School Support)
Legends texts: Agnès Vandewiele
Poster and maps illustrations: Armelle Drouin
Illustrations of the thematical parts: Olivier Verbrugghe
Legends illustrations: Laurent Batteix (The Yeti), Crescence Bouvarel (The Baobab's Treasure),
Pascale Breysse (The Enchanted Caribou), Sylvie Giroire (Catalina and the Whale),
Héloïse Robin (The Amazon Rainforest, The Rainbow Snake)

Graphics and layout: Christelle and Bertrand Defretin and Annaïs Tassone

Translation from French: Susan Allen Maurin
Original title: *Mon premier Atlas*
© Auzou Publishing, Paris (France), 2012 (English version)
ISBN: 978-2-7338-2148-0
All rights reserved. No part of this book may be used or reproduced in any form or by any means,
electronic or mechanical, including photocopying, recording, or by any information storage and
retrieval system, without permission in writing from the publisher.

Printed and bound in China, June 2013.

Contents

Our World

NORTH AMERICA

ATLANTIC OCEAN

Earth is flattened at its top and bottom, called the poles. It bulges at its middle, called the equator.

SOUTH AMERICA

PACIFIC OCEAN

Globes and maps show our world in a smaller version.

A globe is a round model of the world. A map is a drawing of an area that shows many natural and man-made features. The map on these pages shows all the continents and oceans of the world.

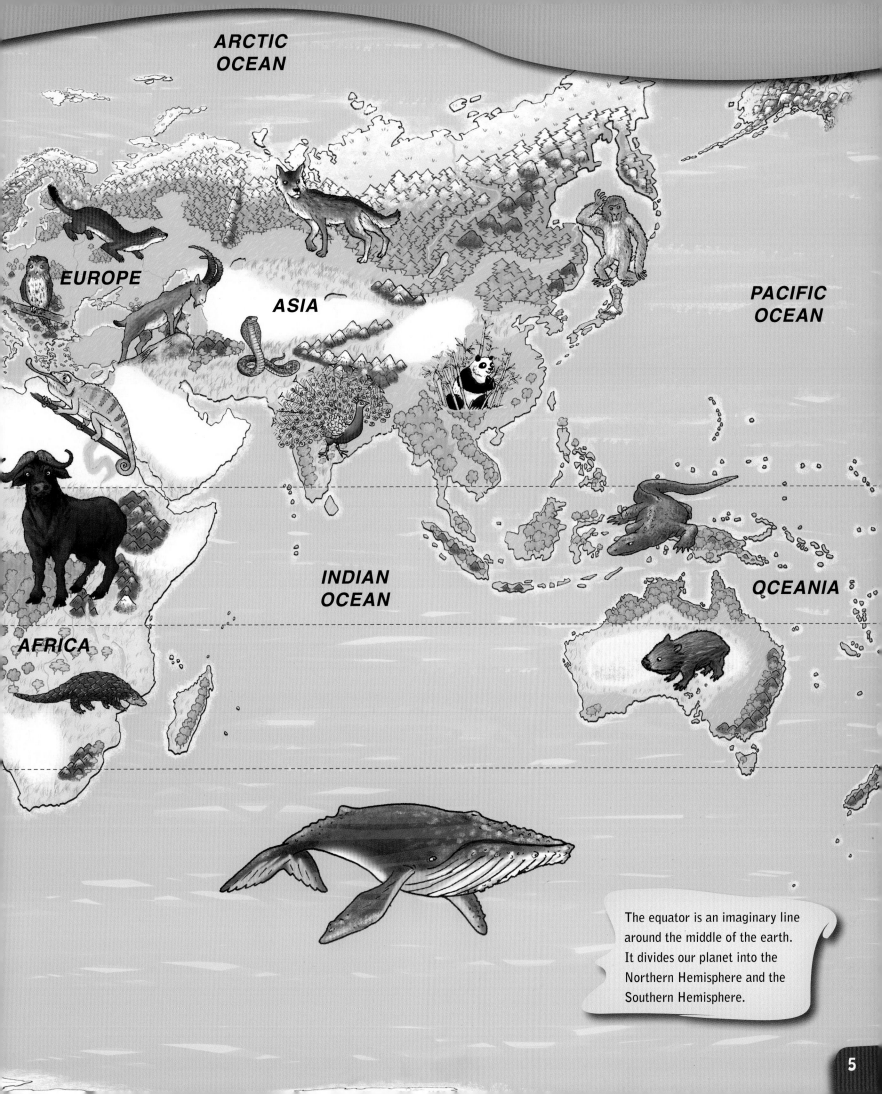

ARCTIC
OCEAN

EUROPE

ASIA

PACIFIC
OCEAN

INDIAN
OCEAN

OCEANIA

AFRICA

The equator is an imaginary line around the middle of the earth. It divides our planet into the Northern Hemisphere and the Southern Hemisphere.

Our World

The earth is one of the eight planets in our solar system. Moving outward from the sun, the planets are Mercury, Venus, Earth, Mars, Jupiter, Saturn, Uranus and Neptune. The planets circle, or orbit, around the sun at different speeds.

The earth is about 93 million miles from the sun (150 million km), which provides our planet with daylight.

From outer space, the earth appears to be blue. That's because three-quarters of our planet is covered by water. Earth is often called the Blue Planet.

Our closest space neighbor is the moon. The moon orbits around the earth. The moon appears to shine in the night sky because its surface reflects the light from the sun.

Day and night occur because the earth spins, or rotates, as it travels around the sun. Half of the planet is lit by the sun's rays while the other half is in darkness. This creates alternating day and night around the world. It takes a little more than 365 days for the earth to travel around the sun. This time is what we call a year.

Earth is also slightly tilted to one side. As our planet orbits around the sun, one hemisphere is closer to the sun. This creates summer in that hemisphere. When the hemisphere is tilted away from the sun, winter occurs.

Earth is made up of seven continents: Africa, North America, South America, Asia, Europe, Oceania and Antarctica.

A continent is a mass of land that contains many different countries. The continents are separated from one another by oceans or large mountain ranges.

To locate places on Earth, we use the four cardinal points, like the ones on a compass. North is at the top, south at the bottom, west to the left and east to the right.

The North Pole is the most northern point on Earth. It lies in the Arctic Ocean. The South Pole is the most southern point, located on the continent of Antarctica.

Deserts cover about one-third of the earth.

The world's four oceans are the Atlantic, the Pacific, the Indian and the Arctic. The Arctic Ocean, in the far north is partially frozen, and forms an ice pack.

There are more than 50 seas on Earth. Some seas are very large, like the Mediterranean Sea. Others are very small, like the Sea of Marmara, near Turkey.

The Pacific Ocean is the world's largest ocean. It is twice the size of the Atlantic Ocean and covers two-thirds of our planet. It is also the deepest ocean: the Marianas Trench is 35,994 feet (10,971 m or 6.8 miles) below sea level.

Our World

Climate

Climate is the weather of a place over a long period of time.

Near the poles, there are only two seasons. In the winter, temperatures can drop to -40° Fahrenheit (-40° Celsius). In the short summers, temperatures rarely go above 68°F (20°C). It is almost always dark in the winter, and in summer, the sun never really sets.

It is always hot in the regions close to the equator, but there is a rainy and dry season. The area of Earth surrounding the equator is called the tropics.

It is always hot in the regions close to the equator, but there is a rainy and dry season. The area of Earth surrounding the equator is called the tropics.

In the deserts, it very rarely or never rains, and life is difficult because of the lack of water. Temperatures can climb above 100°F (38°C) in the day and drop to around 32°F (0°C) at night.

Plants

Different types of plant life thrive in different parts of the world, depending on how much sunlight and water they require.

In dry regions, such as deserts, there is often very little vegetation. In hot and humid climates, there is an abundance of vegetation, often with many plants and dense forests.

Plants are important because they release oxygen into the air for humans and animals to breathe.

Population

There are about 7 billion living people on Earth. Each year, the world's population increases by about 80 million people. On the average, four people are born and two people die every second.

All humans are different and there are many different races of people. Some people are mixed-race. For example, a person born in the United States can have a Latino mother and an African-American father.

Humans live almost everywhere on Earth, but some regions have many more people than others. Towns are generally built along rivers and by the sea to have easy access to water, and often on flat ground to make building easier.

About 100 years ago, one out of ten people lived in cities. Today, one out of two people lives in cities.

The biggest cities in the world are, in order of size: Tokyo (capital of Japan), New York (in the United States of America), Mexico City (capital of Mexico), Seoul (capital of South Korea) and Bombay (in India).

In North America, for example in Canada, many houses are built of wood.

Houses are built differently throughout the world. They are built to suit different weather conditions and the activities of the people living in them. They are also built according to the building materials available in the area.

In Africa, huts are built out of clay (a type of soil) and the roofing is made from straw or from the large leaves of palm trees.

The nomads of Africa and Asia live in tents.

In Europe, houses are often built from concrete and stone, although wooden houses are common in Northern Europe.

Gigantic buildings called skyscrapers are built with modern steel and glass technology. They can often be found in business districts in cities such as New York or in Dubai, in the United Arab Emirates.

Africa

The Land

EUROPE

BLACK SEA

ASIA

GIBRALTAR STRAIT

MEDITERRANEAN SEA

SUEZ CANAL

Atlas Mountains

Nile River

RED SEA

Sahara Desert

Sahel

Senegal River

Niger River

Lake Chad

Lake Assal

Ethiopian Highlands

Lake Turkana

RIFT VALLEY

GULF OF GUINEA

Congo Basin

Lake Victoria

Mount Kilimanjaro (19,341 ft/5,895 m)

Congo River

Lake Tanganyika

INDIAN OCEAN

Lake Malawi

Zambezi River

Lake Kariba

Namib Desert

Kalahari Desert

ATLANTIC OCEAN

Drakensberg

MADAGASCAR

Cape of Good Hope

Africa is the second biggest continent after Asia. It stretches from the Mediterranean Sea to the north to the Cape of Good Hope to the south, and from the Atlantic Ocean to the west to the Indian Ocean to the east.

Africa is a land of contrasts. It is home to the Sahara Desert, the biggest desert in the world, as well as the snowy peaks of the Atlas Mountains and Mount Kilimanjaro. The world's longest river, the Nile, is also in Africa.

0   900 km

Scale

Map of Countries

EUROPE

BLACK SEA

ASIA

MEDITERRANEAN SEA

GIBRALTAR STRAIT

MADEIRA

Alger

Tunis

Rabat

Casablanca

TUNISIA

Tripoli

CANARY ISLANDS

MOROCCO

LIBYA

Cairo

EGYPT

ALGERIA

CAPE VERDE

MAURITANIA

Nouakchott

NIGER

CHAD

SUDAN

Karthoum

RED SEA

ERITREA

Asmara

SENEGAL

Dakar

GAMBIA

Banjul

MALI

Bamako

Niamey

DJIBOUTI

Bissau

GUINEA-BISSAU

GUINEA

BURKINA FASO

Ouagadougou

BENIN

NIGERIA

N'Djamena

Addis Ababa

SOMALIA

Conakry

CÔTE D'IVOIRE

Abuja

SOUTH SUDAN

Juba

ETHIOPIA

Freetown

SIERRA LEONE

TOGO

GHANA

Yamoussoukro

Accra

Lomé

Lagos

Porto-Novo

CENTRAL AFRICAN REPUBLIC

Bangui

Monrovia

LIBERIA

CAMEROON

Yaoundé

Mogadishu

Malabo

SÃO TOMÉ AND PRÍNCIPE

GULF OF GUINEA

Libreville

CONGO

GABON

UGANDA

Kampala

KENYA

Nairobi

SEYCHELLES

EQUATORIAL GUINEA

RWANDA

Kigali

BURUNDI

Bujumbura

Brazzaville

Kinshasa

DEMOCRATIC REPUBLIC OF THE CONGO

TANZANIA

Dodoma

INDIAN OCEAN

The equator and the tropics cross Africa, making the continent generally hot.

Luanda

COMOROS

MAYOTTE

ATLANTIC OCEAN

There are 53 independent countries in Africa.

ZAMBIA

Lusaka

Lilongwe

MALAWI

MADAGASCAR

Antananarivo

MAURITIUS

ANGOLA

Harare

ZIMBABWE

MOZAMBIQUE

MOZAMBIQUE CHANNEL

REUNION

Africa is the second most populated continent in the world. It has a very young average population, with 50 percent of all Africans under 20 years old.

NAMIBIA

BOTSWANA

Windhoek

Gaborone

Pretoria

Maputo

Johannesburg

Lobamba

SWAZILAND

SUEZ CANAL

SOUTH AFRICA

Maseru

LESOTHO

0   900 km

Scale

Le Cap

Cape of Good Hope

11

Africa

The African landscape varies greatly. We can find huge deserts as well as tropical forests and humid and dry savannahs, which are flat, grassy plains with few or no trees. There are very few plants in the Sahel, the region between the Sahara in the north and savannas in the south.

Africa is the world's largest plateau. A plateau is a large, flat open area that is above sea level. The continent is flat at its coastline, but then rapidly rises at about 18½ miles (30 km) from the sea. Unlike the other continents, Africa does not have any high mountain ranges.

The two main mountain peaks are Mount Kilimanjaro at 19,341 feet (5,895 m) and Mount Kenya at 17,057 feet (5,199 m). Lake Victoria, Africa's largest lake, lies close to these mountains. The Nile River is 6,718 miles (4,130 m) long.

The continent also includes islands, such as Madagascar, Zanzibar and the Comoros to the east. Other islands are São Tomé and Príncipe to the west, off the coast of Gabon.

Climate

Africa has many different climates, even though it is generally hot throughout the continent. The climate changes as we move away from the equator.

At the northern tip, by the Mediterranean Sea, summers are hot and dry. The winters are mild with little rain.

From the north to the center of Africa, home to the Sahara and the Namib Deserts, the climate is hot and dry year-round. Along the Atlantic Ocean coast, the climate is milder with a little rain.

Landscape of Mauritius

Landscape of Madagascar

From central Africa to the south and on the islands of the Indian Ocean, such as Mauritius and Madagascar, it is always hot and can rain at any time of the year.

Mount Kilimanjaro

Further south, the seasons are the opposite of what they are in Europe and North America. When it is 41°F (5°C) in Paris, France, in January, temperatures are about 77°F (25°C) in Johannesburg, South Africa. Here, the summers are hot and dry, and the winters are mild and mainly dry.

The peaks of the Atlas Mountain range in the north are covered in snow. Snow is also present on Uhuru peak, the highest point of Mount Kilimanjaro, a collection of three dormant, or "sleeping," volcanoes.

Africa

Plants

In North Africa, which is known as the Maghreb, we find shrubs, bushes and trees such as the date palm, wild olive trees and holm oaks.

Palm Tree

Acacia with Yellow and Pink Flowers

There is little plant life in the African deserts because it rarely rains. It is possible, however, to find shrubs such as acacias with their pink and yellow flowers, and some bushes close to oases, places where water can be found.

Savannas, or grasslands, are common in Africa and are often found at the edge of tropical or equatorial forests. Savannas are big open prairies with tall and thick grass, bushes and a few trees, such as the baobab.

In West Africa, below the Sahara Desert, we find a tropical forest. It consists of large, green-leaved trees and many types of flowers.

An equatorial rainforest occupies much of central Africa. It is similar to a tropical forest but even more dense and humid.

Animals

Crocodile

Crocodiles live in the Nile river, in Egypt.

Bactrian Camel

In the desert, the most common animals are the Arabian camel (with one hump) and the Bactrian camel (with two humps), fennec foxes and the addax antelope.

Many animals live in the savanna, such as the African elephant with its long ears, the rhinoceros, the giraffe and many types of big cat such as the lion and the leopard.

In tropical forests and rainforests, there are hippopotamuses, many different birds with brightly colored feathers, insects, reptiles and monkeys such as the gorilla and chimpanzee.

Lemurs are found on the island of Madagascar. These animals have a long nose, big eyes and a long tail that allows them to hang from trees.

Lemur

History and Population

There are two main families of African people: the inhabitants of the Maghreb (Morocco, Algeria and Tunisia) and north of the Sahara, who have light skin, and the people from south of the Sahara, who have very dark skin.

The people of North Africa have been in contact with their Asian and European neighbors for thousands of years. Before the construction of the Suez Canal, in Egypt, 150 years ago, it was possible to travel from Egypt to Asia and from Asia to Europe by foot.

For many years, South and Central Africa were isolated from the rest of the world. Merchants only came ashore to trade and take slaves. Today, the rich culture of Africa is known worldwide.

At one time, almost all of Africa was colonized by European nations, such as France, Great Britain and Belgium. People from these nations settled in Africa and controlled life throughout the continent. Today, almost all African nations are independent, but many still speak the language of the colonial power.

Some of the largest cities in Africa are Cairo in Egypt, Casablanca in Morocco and Lagos in Nigeria.

In many parts of Africa, people live in poverty, struggling to find enough food and clean water. Long dry spells that destroy crops, disease and war are also common.

South Africa has much wealth in its gold and diamond mines and its rivers.

Pyramids of Giza

In Egypt, there are magnificent monuments that show the skill of the ancient people: the pyramids of Giza and temples, such as Karnak.

Karnak Temple

Africa

Customs

There are many cultural traditions practiced in Africa. In the Maghreb, people eat couscous, a type of grain, during celebrations. Weddings are huge parties that often last for days. Women decorate their hands with a type of dye known as henna. Most men and women wear a *djellaba*, a long dress that covers their entire body.

The tuaregs live in the Sahara. They are known as the "blue people" because they wear large blue headscarves to protect themselves from the sun and the blowing desert sand. They are nomadic, or wandering, people, traveling mainly on camel.

In central Africa, different tribes are known for their handsome statues and sculptures that pay tribute to their gods and ancestors.

Africans love dancing: for any big event, people dance around the fire to the sound of drums.

Off the coast of islands such as the Seychelles, people swim year-round in clear water filled with multicolored fish.

Many Africans move to the cities in search of work and better housing. As the cities get more crowded, however, many become shantytowns. These are slums where poor people often live in housing made from scrap materials such as cardboard and plastic.

Quick Quiz

Test your knowledge on Africa... to help you, the answers are on the page in the form of drawings.

1 Kilimanjaro is one. It is not extinct, it's dormant.

2 The world's biggest desert.

3 Women decorate their hands with this.

4 Where do the gorilla and chimpanzee live?

5 Grassy plains where the lions, giraffes and zebras live...

6 A tree that grows on these grassy plains.

7 We say that he is the "king of animals."

8 The traditional dress in the Maghreb.

9 My name is Victoria, what am I?

10 An animal from Madagascar that is part of the monkey family.

→ Solutions page 78

The Baobab's Treasure

Under a scorching hot sun, Hare ran across the savanna. Suddenly, he saw a baobab tree, sat back against its trunk and exclaimed:
"How refreshing the shade of this baobab tree is!"
He leapt up in surprise when a voice replied:
"My shade is nice, but my monkey bread fruits are even better!"
He was surprised to hear Baobab talking to him.
"Would you like to taste a monkey bread?"
"Yes, please," replied Hare.
So Baobab let a perfectly ripe monkey bread fruit drop to the ground.
Hare ate the thirst-quenching fruit.
"That was delicious!" he said.
"You thought my monkey bread was delicious," said Baobab, "but what you'll find inside my trunk is a thousand times better."
"May I see what's inside your trunk?" asked Hare.
"Because you liked my shade and my monkey bread, I'll let you look inside my trunk. You can even take whatever you want!"

The baobab's trunk opened. Hare climbed inside and was blinded by piles of gold, silver and precious jewels. Hare took some of the treasure, thanked Baobab and returned home, overjoyed. While Hare's family were admiring the wealth, Hyena's wife, their neighbor, came to visit.

She saw the treasure and quickly ran home to tell her husband.
"How did Hare come by such treasure?" asked Hyena, jealously.
He jumped up and ran round to ask his neighbor:
"Where did you find such a fortune?"
"In the trunk of a baobab tree", said Hare.
"Take me to this baobab tree!" ordered Hyena.

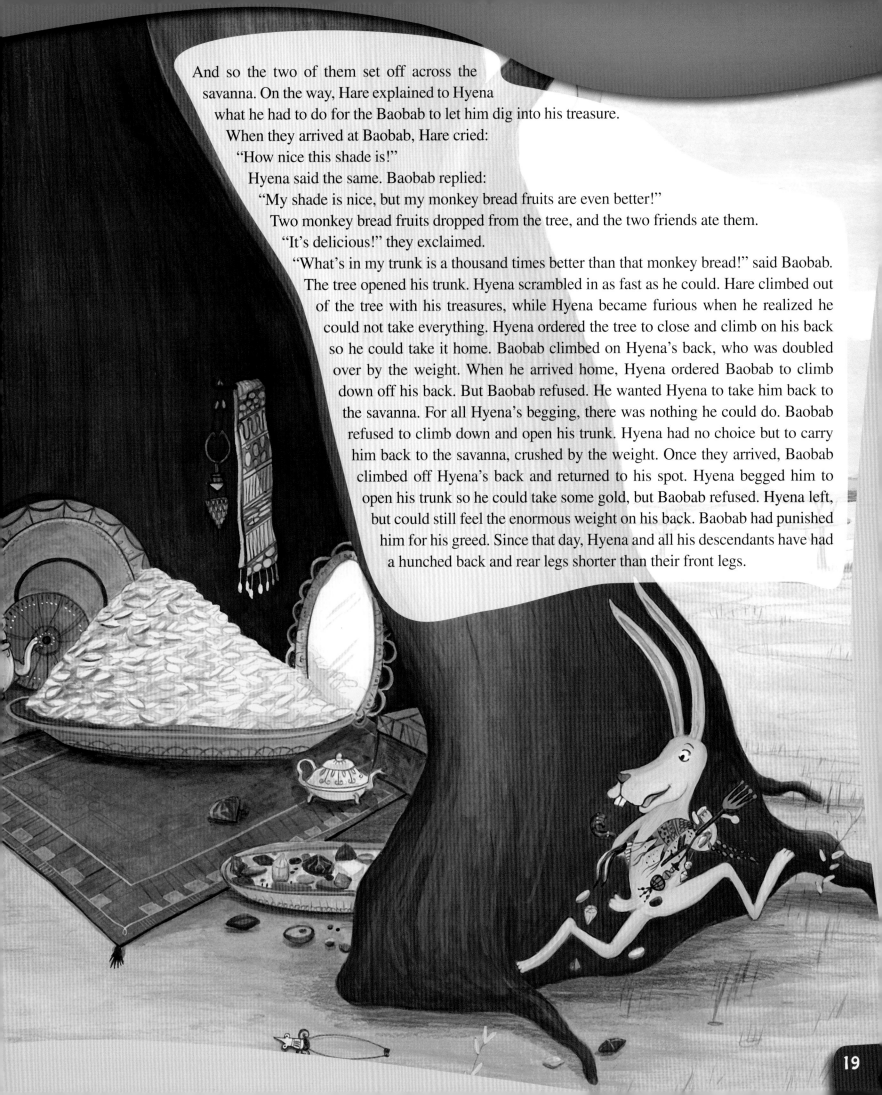

And so the two of them set off across the savanna. On the way, Hare explained to Hyena what he had to do for the Baobab to let him dig into his treasure.

When they arrived at Baobab, Hare cried:

"How nice this shade is!"

Hyena said the same. Baobab replied:

"My shade is nice, but my monkey bread fruits are even better!"

Two monkey bread fruits dropped from the tree, and the two friends ate them.

"It's delicious!" they exclaimed.

"What's in my trunk is a thousand times better than that monkey bread!" said Baobab. The tree opened his trunk. Hyena scrambled in as fast as he could. Hare climbed out of the tree with his treasures, while Hyena became furious when he realized he could not take everything. Hyena ordered the tree to close and climb on his back so he could take it home. Baobab climbed on Hyena's back, who was doubled over by the weight. When he arrived home, Hyena ordered Baobab to climb down off his back. But Baobab refused. He wanted Hyena to take him back to the savanna. For all Hyena's begging, there was nothing he could do. Baobab refused to climb down and open his trunk. Hyena had no choice but to carry him back to the savanna, crushed by the weight. Once they arrived, Baobab climbed off Hyena's back and returned to his spot. Hyena begged him to open his trunk so he could take some gold, but Baobab refused. Hyena left, but could still feel the enormous weight on his back. Baobab had punished him for his greed. Since that day, Hyena and all his descendants have had a hunched back and rear legs shorter than their front legs.

North America

ARCTIC OCEAN

ASIA

BERING SEA

BERING STRAIT

BEAUFORT SEA

GREENLAND (Denmark)

BAFFIN BAY

Yukon

Mount McKinley (20,320 ft/6,914 m)

Mackenzie

Great Bear Lake

LABRADOR SEA

GULF OF ALASKA

R O C K Y   M O U N T A I N S

Great Slave Lake

HUDSON BAY

North America forms the largest part of the Americas. It stretches from the Arctic Ocean in the north, to the Isthmus of Panama, a narrow strip of land in the south of Central America, with the Atlantic Ocean to the east and the Pacific Ocean to the west.

Athabasca

Lake Winnepeg

Missouri R.

Lake Superior

Lake Huron

Lake Michigan

Lake Ontario

Lake Erie

Great Salt Lake

CENTRAL AMERICA

Mississippi R.

Ohio R.

ATLANTIC OCEAN

Colorado R.

Grand Canyon

PACIFIC OCEAN

Rio Grande R.

GULF OF MEXICO

ANTILLES

CARIBBEAN SEA

PANAMA CANAL

SOUTH AMERICA

0   900 km
Scale

Map of Countries

The continent of North America includes 22 independent countries.

ARCTIC OCEAN

GREENLAND (Denmark)

NUNAVUT

ATLANTIC OCEAN

YUKON

NORTHWEST TERRITORIES

BRITISH COLUMBIA

HUDSON BAY

NEWFOUNDLAND AND LABRADOR

UNITED STATES
1- ALABAMA
2- ALASKA
3- ARIZONA
4- ARKANSAS
5- CALIFORNIA
6- NORTH CAROLINA
7- SOUTH CAROLINA
8- COLORADO
9- CONNECTICUT
10- NORTH DAKOTA
11- SOUTH DAKOTA
12- DELAWARE
13- FLORIDA
14- GEORGIA
15- HAWAII
16- IDAHO
17- ILLINOIS
18- INDIANA
19- IOWA
20- KANSAS
21- KENTUCKY
22- LOUISIANA
23- MAINE
24- MARYLAND
25- MASSACHUSETTS
26- MICHIGAN
27- MINNESOTA
28- MISSISSIPPI
29- MISSOURI
30- MONTANA
31- NEBRASKA
32- NEVADA
33- NEW HAMPSHIRE
34- NEW JERSEY
35- NEW YORK
36- NEW MEXICO
37- OHIO
38- OKLAHOMA
39- OREGON
40- PENNSYLVANIA
41- RHODE ISLAND
42- TENNESSEE
43- TEXAS
44- UTAH
45- VERMONT
46- VIRGINIA
47- WEST VIRGINIA
48- WASHINGTON
49- WISCONSIN
50- WYOMING

ALBERTA

SASKATCHEWAN

MANITOBA

ONTARIO

QUEBEC

Montreal

Ottawa

Vancouver

PRINCE EDWARD ISLAND

NEW BRUNSWICK

NOVA SCOTIA

48
30
39
16
50
10
27
49
26
35
23
33
45
Boston
25
9
41
San Francisco
32
44
8
31
19
18
37
40
34
12
New-York
Chicago
17
24
Washington DC
5
20
29
47
46
3
36
38
4
28
21
42
6
Los Angeles
Dallas
22
1
14
7
43

LESSER ANTILLES
1- ANTIGUA AND BARBUDA
2- BARBADOS
3- DOMINICA
4- GRENADA
5- SAINT LUCIA
6- SAINT KITTS AND NEVIS
7- SAINT VINCENT AND THE GRENADINES
8- TRINIDAD AND TOBAGO

13
Miami

BAHAMAS

CARIBBEAN SEA

PACIFIC OCEAN

Havana

CUBA

Puerto Rico (United States)

HAITI

JAMAICA

Kingston

DOMINICAN REPUBLIC

Guadeloupe (France)

Martinique (France)

MEXICO

3350 miles
HAWAII
5400 km

Mexico City

0   900 km
Scale

BELIZE
Belmopan

GUATEMALA
Guatemala City

HONDURAS
Tegucigalpa

PANAMA CANAL

San Salvador
SALVADOR

NICARAGUA
Managua

Panama City

San José
COSTA RICA

PANAMA

SOUTH AMERICA

North America

North America offers a wide variety of landscapes.

North America has huge lakes such as Lake Michigan, in the United States, and Lake Superior, on the border of the United States and Canada. Lake Superior is the world's largest freshwater lake.

Here we find mountain ranges such as the Appalachians, to the east of the continent, and the Rocky Mountains, which run down the western side from Alaska to Mexico.

Many long rivers run throughout the continent. The Niagara River flows on the border of the United States and Canada. Its enormous waterfall is known as Niagara Falls.

The Colorado River is found in the southwest of the United States. It runs through a vast gorge called the Grand Canyon, which was formed by erosion millions of years ago.

Many volcanoes, both active and extinct, are found in North America and on the Antilles Islands, such as Mount Garibaldi in Canada or La Soufriere on the island of Guadeloupe. Central America is also a volcanic region.

Climate

Throughout northern Canada and Alaska, as well as Greenland, winters are long and summers are short. It is very cold in these areas, which are covered in snow and ice nearly all the year.

Further inland in Canada and Alaska, down to the United States border, it is cold and snows a lot in the winter. Summers are cool and a little humid.

In the United States and northern Mexico, summers are hot and winters cool. It rains regularly throughout the year.

South of the Rocky Mountains, inland of the western United States and western Mexico, the climate is hot and dry.

From southern Mexico as far as the Panama Canal, and on the Antilles Islands, it is hot and humid throughout the year. During the summer, these regions often experience violent storms with very strong winds.

Plants

Lichen

The boreal forest crosses Canada and Alaska from west to east. It is made up of conifer trees, meaning trees of the pine family.

The frozen land of the northern edge of the continent is covered by tundra, where moss and lichen are the most common plants.

In mountain ranges such as the Sierra Nevada in California, we find forests of huge redwood or sequoia trees. These enormous trees can grow up to 380 feet (115 m) high.

Many types of cactus grow in the desert regions of the western United States and northern Mexico.

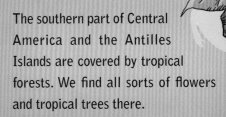

The southern part of Central America and the Antilles Islands are covered by tropical forests. We find all sorts of flowers and tropical trees there.

Tropical Flowers

North America

Animals

Polar Bear

Because of its varied climate, the American continent contains many different types of animal.

Raccoon

In the boreal forest, we find wolves, brown bears, grizzly bears, beavers, raccoons and many types of deer, such as caribou.

The polar bear lives on the frozen coastlines of Canada, Alaska and Greenland. It is the world's biggest land carnivore, or meat eater, dining on fish and seals.

The American alligator and the American crocodile live in the wetlands of Florida, in the United States.

Bison

Rattlesnake

The vast plains in the center of the continent contain hares, bison and prairie dogs, a type of rodent. Coyotes and rattlesnakes are also found here.

The golden eagle is the biggest bird in the eagle family. It lives in the mountainous regions of the continent.

Hummingbird

Many different birds live in the tropical forests of Central America and on the Antilles Islands. These include the hummingbird and the toucan, with its brightly colored bead, and many types of parrots.

Swordfish

Toucan

There are many types of fish and marine mammals in the waters around North America, including the whale and the swordfish, named after its swordlike bill.

Whale

Many national parks have been created in the North America, such as Yellowstone National Park, in order to protect endangered plants and animals.

History and Population

The American people have many different origins. Native Americans, or American Indians, are descendants of people from Asia. The Inuits of the Arctic region were the first inhabitants of the continent.

The number of American Indians has decreased and their lives have been modernized since the arrival of Europeans. Many American Indians now live on reservations like the ones in Oklahoma, situated in the center of the United States.

There are roughly 2.9 million American Indians living in the United States today. Some live on reservations, areas of land managed by Native American tribes under the supervision of the U.S. government. Some researchers believe that centuries ago there were as many as 18 million Native Americans living in North America.

Slaves brought from Africa to North America were the ancestors of African-Americans. Today, African-Americans make up about 14 percent of the U.S. population.

English is the main language spoken in the United States and Canada. French is also spoken in Quebec, a Canadian province. Spanish is the most widely spoken language in Central America.

The first inhabitants of Central America were the Mayas and the Aztecs, also known as "People of the Sun." They lived in large cities built of stone. The Maya and Aztec civilizations disappeared after their lands were conquered by the Spanish army.

New York City, in the northeast part of the United States, is the second most populated city in the world, behind Tokyo, Japan.

The Spanish, French, Russians and English were early explorers of the present-day United States.

Mount Rushmore in the state of South Dakota is a man-made sculpture of four U.S. presidents who shaped America's history: Lincoln, Theodore Roosevelt, Jefferson and Washington.

Mount Rushmore

Customs

The people of Alaska often have dog sled races. The most famous is the Iditarod Race, run each year in March. The teams of dogs and drivers cover about 1,150 miles (1,850 km) in the frigid cold.

Football is one of the most popular sports in the United States. Each week, millions of viewers watch their favorite teams play on television. Football is also widely played in Canada.

Hamburger

The famous hamburger was invented in the United States.

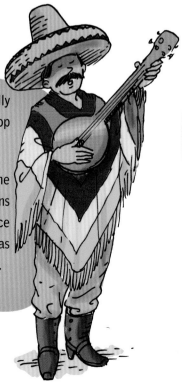

The sombrero is a hat traditionally worn in Mexico. It is high on top of the head with a wide brim.

It protects the wearer from the sun and the heat. Some Mexicans wear ponchos. This colorful piece of clothing has no sleeves and has a hole to put the head through.

The rumba comes from the island of Cuba, in the Antilles. It is a type of music combining singing and drums, where the rythm starts off slowly and speeds up. It is a very popular dance.

The year is 1855. Nagawika has been out hunting for his tribe. Can you help him find his way back home to his village?

→ Solution page 78

Legend

The Enchanted Caribou

Close to a lake in the Great North, lived a young woman named Ava. She was walking along the river bank searching for wood to make dolls. One day, she strayed far away from the camp and found herself in a thick fog. Thinking she was lost, she began to cry.

Suddenly, she sensed a presence close by.

A figure approached, and she saw it was a man.

"What are you doing here?" he asked her.

"I was collecting wood and the mist surprised me. I'm completely lost."

"Come with me," said the man. "My name is Katak." He took Ava to his tent.

When Katak's two brothers arrived home, they were surprised to see their brother with a young woman. Like Katak, they were caribou hunters. Before going to sleep, they put on a caribou mask and did a ritual dance, asking the spirits for a good hunt the next day. Ava danced with them. Early the next morning, the three brothers warned Ava not to let anyone into the tent. Yet, shortly after they had left, an old woman appeared and asked her:

"Please, let me come in and have a glass of water."

"I can't," said Ava. "Katak and his brothers told me not to let anyone in."

"If you refuse, you will be cursed, as I am a shaman," replied the old lady.

Ava knew that a shaman possessed magical powers, so she let her in and poured her a drink. The old woman then asked to brush her hair with a magical comb. She hummed a song so soothing that Ava fell asleep, and the old woman disappeared. When she awoke, Ava felt her body transforming. Antlers were growing on her head, her legs were becoming longer and her feet were transforming into hooves. She had become a white caribou! During the hunt, Katak had never stopped thinking about Ava. On returning home, the young man and his brothers saw that she had disappeared. That night, Katak dreamed of his grandmother, who was a shaman.

South America

CARIBBEAN SEA

CENTRAL AMERICA

Panama Canal

Orinoco R.

Galapagos Islands (Ecuador)

Amazon R.

Amazon rainforest

Lake Titicaca

ANDES MOUNTAINS

Aconcagua (22,841 ft/6,962 m)

Tocantins R.

PACIFIC OCEAN

Parana R.

PAMPA

Uruguay R.

Rio de la Plata

ATLANTIC OCEAN

South America is almost as large as North America. It stretches from southern Panama in the north to Cape Horn, the southern tip of the continent, and between the Pacific Ocean to the west and the Atlantic Ocean in the east.

Strait of Magellan

Tierra del Fuego

Cape Horn

0   900 km

Scale

Map of Countries

CARIBBEAN SEA

CENTRAL AMERICA

Caracas

VENEZUELA

Georgetown
GUYANA
Paramaribo
SURINAM
Cayenne
GUYANE
(FRENCH GUYANA)

Bogotá

COLOMBIA

Quito
ECUADOR

Galapagos Islands (Ecuador)

PERU

Lima

BRAZIL

Recife

Salvador

Brasilia

La Paz
BOLIVIA

Belo Horizonte

PARAGUAY

CHILI

Rio de Janeiro
Sao Paulo

Asunción

Porto Alegre

ATLANTIC OCEAN

URUGUAY

PACIFIC OCEAN

Santiago

Buenos Aires

Montevideo

ARGENTINA

South America is made up of 13 independent countries. Brazil and Argentina are among the largest countries in the world. South America, however, is not very highly populated considering its size, because a large part of the continent is covered by the Amazon rainforest.

FALKLAND ISLANDS
(GREAT BRITAIN)

0   900 km
Scale

Ushuaia

South America

Much of South America remains wild and uninhabited, although there are some large cities on the coasts. In central South America there are large open plains. In the south there are fertile grasslands called the Pampas.

The Andes Mountains run down the entire west side of South America along the Pacific coast. It is the world's largest mountain range. It measures about 4,300 miles (7,250 km) long. The highest peak is Aconcagua at 22,841 feet (6,962 m), the tallest peak outside the Himalayas in Asia.

There are very few big lakes in South America, apart from Lake Maracaibo, in Venezuela, and Titicaca split between Peru and Bolivia.

The Amazon is the world's second longest river at 3,976 miles (6,392 km) long. It is the only large river in the world with no bridges across it. There are also other smaller rivers like the Iguazu, known for its waterfalls on the Brazilian and Argentinian border.

Angel Falls, the world's biggest waterfall, is in Venezuela. It measures 3,212 feet (979 m) high.

Climate

Every different type of climate can be found in South America.

From the north to the center of the continent, where there is the Amazon jungle, it is hot and humid all year round.

From the center of the continent to the south, in the Pampas, winters are mild and the summers hot and humid.

South America also has some deserts where it rarely rains and is very hot.

The highest summits and the far south are covered in snow and ice all year round.

Plants

The world's biggest tropical forest is the Amazon rainforest, which produces much of the world's oxygen. This wild region is in danger as man cuts down the trees for wood, to grow crops or build roads.

In the high mountains of the Andes, there are few plants. However, potatoes were discovered here and are now grown everywhere.

In Chili, there are vines that produce wine that is sold around the world.

In southern Brazil, we find a region of steppes, a type of dry grassland. Below that, there are big areas of prarie, like the Argentinian Pampas. The people there grow crops and raise animals.

In the cold desert regions of Patagonia, in the southernmost part of the continent, there are very few plants as it rarely rains. The only plants are moss and lichen.

South America

Animals

Hummingbird

Giant Anteater

In the Amazon rainforest, we find many types of insects, butterflies and snakes, such as the anaconda. Birds include toucans and hummingbirds. Leopards and different types of monkeys also live here. The giant anteater, who eats ants with the help of his long tongue, and the sloth also live in this tree-covered area.

Tapir

Armadillo

In the Pampas grasslands, we find the tapir, who has a type of snout to eat with. The armadillo, whose back is covered with bony plates that resemble a knight's armor, also lives in this area.

Throughout the Andes, we find the chinchilla, a small nocturnal rodent, and the lama. The Quechua people, descendants of the Incas, raise sheep and lamas on the high plateaus between the mountains.

The rivers and streams are home to many types of fish, including the piranha, a meat-eating fish.

Lama

Chinchilla

Giant Tortoise

The giant tortoise lies on Galapados Islands in the Pacific Ocean.

History and Population

The Indians of South America were given their name by Christopher Columbus.
Sailing from Portugal, Columbus thought he had traveled around the world and arrived in India when he landed on an island in the Caribbean Sea. Indians who are descended from the people of Asia still live in the forests of South America.

This region was marked by the Inca Empire, which occupied an area now spread between Peru, Bolivia, Argentina and Colombia.
The Inca people were well organized and technologically advanced. We still have many traces of their magnificent artwork in the beautiful gold carvings and ruins of their palaces in cities such as Cuzco, their capital, and Machu Picchu.
The descendants of slaves brought from Africa to work in the mines and the fields live around the Caribbean Sea. Most of the people in the Americas today are of European origin. In South America, people are mainly of Spanish and Portuguese origin.

The whole continent has Spanish as its official language, except Brazil, which uses Portuguese.
A huge part of South America is very sparsely populated: 3 out of 4 people live in the cities along the coast. The biggest cities are Sao Paulo and Rio de Janeiro, in Brazil, followed by Buenos Aires in Argentina. Many areas of South America are quite poor despite an abundance of natural resources. Life is often difficult.

South America

Customs

In Brazil, people love soccer, music and samba, a very popular dance. Tourists come from around the world to admire the musicians and dancers during the Rio Carnival. It takes place every year for Mardi Gras and lasts 5 days.

In Argentina, people dance the tango, which was born in Buenos Aires over a 100 years ago. A man and woman dance together to the music of the bandoneon, a type of accordian, the violin and the piano.

In the Pampas, we find gauchos. They are horsemen who look after the herds of animals in the big open plains. They work on enormous ranches.

The only territory on the continent that remains a colony is French Guiana, an overseas department of France. In Kourou, there is the European Space agency base from where the Ariane rockets are launched.

In the Andes, musicians play traditional songs on pan flutes, guitars and drums in traditional colorful costumes. Locals wear ponchos and hat; women wear big skirts to work in the fields.

Riddles

1

My **first part** is the first letter of the compass point opposite of south.
My **second part** is another word for me.
My **third part** is a popular type of transportation.
My **fourth part** is the Spanish word for water.
My **whole** is a country in Central America between Honduras and Costa Rica.

2

My **first part** is what I eat my breakfast cereal from, minus "W."
My **second part** is the letter that follows H in the alphabet.
My **third part** means "by way of."

3

I am the country where the tango was invented. Which country am I?

4

I am one of the horsemen who watches the great herds on the Pampas. What am I?

5

I am the capital of the biggest country in South America. Who am I?

→ Solutions page 78

The Amazon Rainforest

A huge sadness filled the Amazon rainforest when the great chief Iaia learned that his son had been killed in battle. Iaia wanted to offer him a burial service worthy of his rank. For 7 days and 7 nights, the women of the village watched over his body and cried, praising his exploits:

"The son of our great chief is dead, he who was the bravest of all, who was the best hunter and the best fisherman in our tribe!"

While the men drank chicha, a traditional drink made from fermented cassava, the musicians played the drums.

The young warrior had been adorned with necklaces of animal teeth and feathers, his body had been covered in annatto, a vegetable paint, and red patterns had been drawn on his face. His father, the chief Iaia, did not want his body to be thrown in the river, or buried in the red earth of the forest. So he went into his garden and took an enormous pumpkin. He scooped out the flesh, keeping only the skin, and placed the body of his son inside. He then said to the elders of his tribe:

"Let us place this in the center of the forest. Let the armadillo and the ants dig his grave, and the toucan sing songs in his memory."

The pumpkin was placed in the middle of a bush and decorated with feathers and pearl necklaces.

The jaguar, the sloth and the peccary watched over the tomb all night. At dawn the next day, Iaia went to visit his son's grave. The pumpkin was still in the same place. Yet, to his astonishment, life was flourishing around it. All around there were shells, little crabs, algae and marine plants clustered together, and in the middle was water filled with multicolored fish. Iaia could not believe his eyes. He quickly returned to the village and told people of the miracle. The forest gods who oversee life and death had created this abundance of plants and fish next to the young warrior's tomb. The people of the village had a spectacular catch of fish the next few days.

But one young man of the tribe, the boldest of them all, wanted to keep the magic pumpkin for himself. He seized the pumpkin, but its weight made him stumble. He began to drag the pumpkin. As he advanced, he realized his load was becoming lighter. He turned around and saw a stream of water coming from the pumpkin. This stream was becoming bigger, transforming into a river and digging a channel through the thick forest, sweeping away the huts, trees and rocks in its passage. The river made a long meander across the country and came crashing into the Atlantic Ocean. The Amazon, king of rivers, was born. Since then the fish-filled waters of the sea-river feed the Indians and Caboclos who live on its banks. When they are lucky, they catch an arapaima, a giant fish that can feed the whole village!

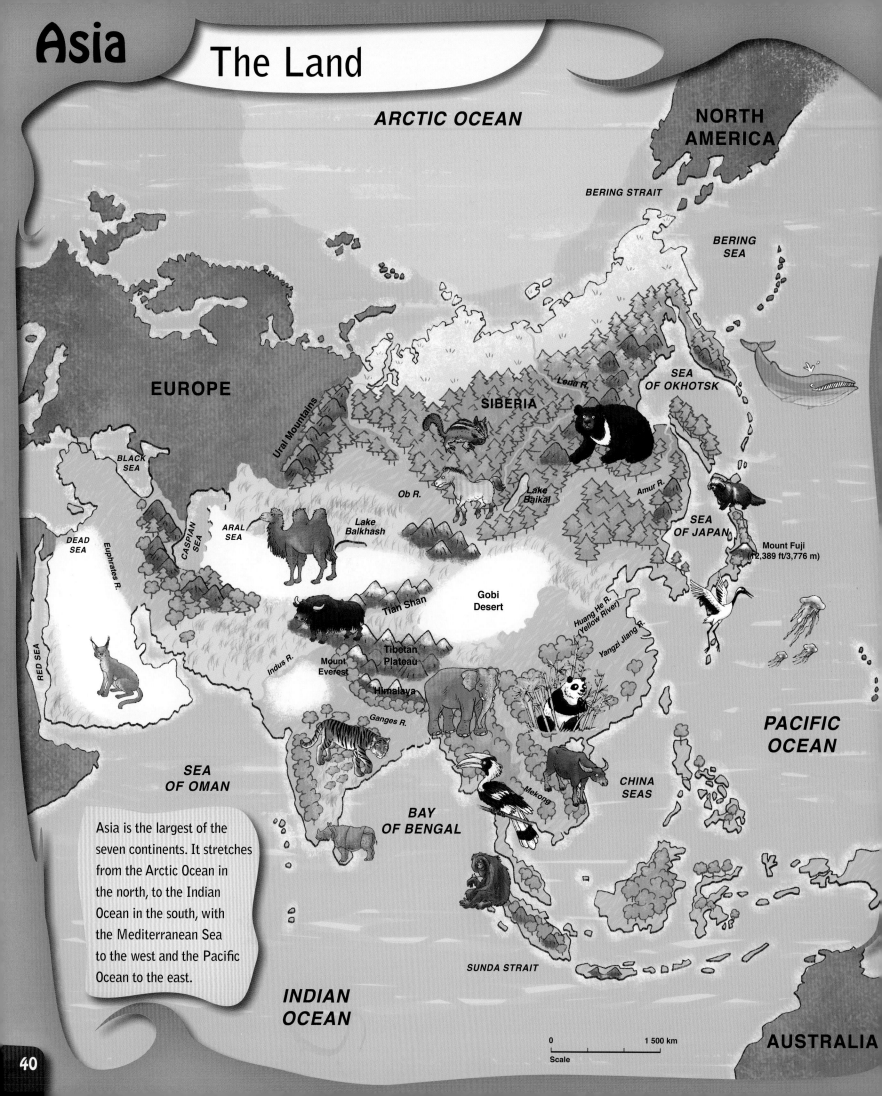

Asia

The Land

ARCTIC OCEAN

NORTH AMERICA

BERING STRAIT

BERING SEA

EUROPE

SIBERIA

Lena R.

SEA OF OKHOTSK

Ural Mountains

Ob R.

Lake Baikal

Amur R.

SEA OF JAPAN

Mount Fuji (12,389 ft/3,776 m)

BLACK SEA

ARAL SEA

Lake Balkhash

CASPIAN SEA

DEAD SEA

Euphrates R.

RED SEA

Tian Shan

Gobi Desert

Huang He R. (Yellow River)

Yangzi Jiang R.

Tibetan Plateau

Mount Everest

Indus R.

Himalaya

Ganges R.

SEA OF OMAN

Mekong

CHINA SEAS

PACIFIC OCEAN

BAY OF BENGAL

Asia is the largest of the seven continents. It stretches from the Arctic Ocean in the north, to the Indian Ocean in the south, with the Mediterranean Sea to the west and the Pacific Ocean to the east.

SUNDA STRAIT

INDIAN OCEAN

0   1 500 km
Scale

AUSTRALIA

Map of countries

NORTH AMERICA

Asia is the heaviest populated continent, with more than 4 billion inhabitants. There are five main geographical zones in Asia: Western Asia, Central Asia, East Asia, South Asia and Southeast Asia. The zones are formally known as the Middle East, Central Asia, the Far East, the Indian Subcontinent and Southeast Asia.

EUROPE

Moscow

RUSSIA

Ankara

Tbilisi
GEORGIA
ARMENIA
TURKEY   Yerevan   AZERBAIJAN
LEBANON   Baku
Beirut
Jerusalem   SYRIA
ISRAEL   Damascus
Palestine   Amman   IRAQ
JORDAN   Baghdad

Astana

KAZAKHSTAN

UZBEKISTAN
Ashgabat   Tashkent   Bishkek
TURKMENISTAN   KYRGYZSTAN
Tehran   TAJIKISTAN
                    Dushanbe

Ulaanbaatar

MONGOLIA

KUWAIT
Manama
Riyadh   BAHRAIN
QATAR   Doha
         Abu Dhabi
SAUDI   UNITED ARAB
ARABIA   EMIRATES
         Muscat
Sana'a' YEMEN   OMAN

IRAN

AFGHANISTAN
Kabul

Islamabad

PAKISTAN

Karachi

New Delhi

NEPAL
Kathmandu   BHUTAN
            Thimphu
INDIA   BANGLADESH
Calcutta   Dhaka

Mumbai

SEA OF OMAN

CHINA

Peking

NORTH KOREA
Pyongyang
SOUTH KOREA   Seoul

JAPAN
Tokyo
Osaka

Shanghai

Taipei

PACIFIC OCEAN

MYANMAR
Nay Pyi Taw
LAOS
Ventiane
THAILAND   VIETNAM
Bangkok
CAMBODIA
Phnom Penh

Hanoi

BAY OF BENGAL

Male
MALDIVES   SRI LANKA
Colombo

PHILIPPINES
Manila

BRUNEI
Bandar Seri Begawan

Kuala Lumpur   MALAYSIA

SINGAPORE

INDONESIA

Dili   EAST TIMOR

INDONESIA
Jakarta

INDIAN OCEAN

AUSTRALIA

0   1 500 km
Scale

Asia

Asia is a continent of extreme landforms.

Here we find the Himalayas, the highest point on Earth's surface. This mountain range features Mount Everest, the world's tallest peak, which stands at 29,029 feet (8,848 m) tall. It is often called "The Roof of the World".

In Asia, we also find the lowest point on Earth's surface. At this point, sea level is much higher than the land. The banks of the Dead Sea, on the border of Israel and Jordan, are 1,388 feet (423 m) below sea level.

Asia is home to the deepest parts of the world's oceans. The Mariana Trench in the Pacific Ocean is 36,168 feet (11,031 m) below sea level.

The Asian continent also includes many big islands such as Japan, Indonesia, Malaysia, the Philippines and Singapore as well as much smaller ones like Maldives.

Asia also has many well-known volcanoes, both on land and in the sea, which are still active: they can erupt and some are constantly erupting, like Mount Merapi in Java, Indonesia, or Mount Fuji in Japan.

Mount Merapi Erupting

Mount Popa

There are also dormant, or "sleeping," volcanoes such as Mount Popa in Myanmar, and extinct ones such as Mount Aragats in Armenia.

Climate

The northern part of Asia, from western Siberia to the north Pacific Ocean, as well as the Tibetan plateau and other high mountain regions, have long and harsh winters. Temperatures drop below -5°F (15°C). Summers are short and cool, with temperatures above 68°F (20°C).

In the center of the continent we find big deserts such as the Gobi Desert. In some countries, such as Syria, Jordan and Yemen, the weather is very cold in winter and very hot in summer. There too, it rarely rains.

In southern Asia it is hot year-round with frequent rain in the summer and less in the winter. In the southeast of the continent, close to Oceania, Indonesia and the Philippines it rains year-round!

East Asia has hot and rainy weather in the summer but cold and damp weather in the winter.

The south and east of the continent often experience violent storms with strong winds during the summer.

The countries in the west of the continent, around the Mediterranean Sea, have a temperate climate, meaning hot and dry in the summer yet mild and humid in winter.

The northern edge of the continent is covered in tundra (where moss and lichen are the main plants) and taiga (big forests of conifers: trees of the same family as pine trees).

Plants

On the boundary of Russia and Mongolia are enormous steppes, which are big grassy plains where nomads raise their herds of animals.

Heading toward the center and west of the continent, the plains are replaced by large deserts and high mountain ranges.

Eucalyptus

Bamboo

The southern and eastern regions, close to the rivers and oceans, are covered in tropical forest. These areas are very green and rich in trees, plants and flowers such as bamboo, oak and eucalyptus.

Asia

Animals

As the Asian climate and vegetation are very varied, we find a wide variety of different animals in Asia.

In the north of Siberia, we find caribous or reindeers, who feed mainly on moss and lichen, as well as many types of arctic birds like the Siberian crane. These birds travel long distances. As soon as winter approaches, they migrate south to Japan, where the weather is warmer.

Further south, in the conifer forests, we find fur-covered animals such as the brown bear and the fox.

Siberian Tiger

Towards the center, in the plains of Mongolia, we find many domesticated herds of animals like horse and sheep, as well as antelope and other wild animals.

The largest member of the cat family, the Siberian Tiger, lives over a large area of land on the Russian and Korean border.

Yak

The yak lives in the mountains of Tibet. He is part of the family of ruminants like cows, which live mainly on grass and moss.

Wild giant pandas are now only found in the bamboo forests of western China.

Tanuki

In the east of Asia, mainly on the edge of Russia, in Korea, North Vietnam, eastern China and Japan, we find the raccoon dog, or tanuki, as the Japanese call it.

44

In the desert regions of Western Asia, the most common animals are the two-humped Bactrian camel and the single-humped Arabian camel. The Caracal ("black cat" in Turkish), also known as the desert lynx or Persian lynx, also lives here.

Lynx

Monkeys

In the countries and islands of Southern and Western Asia, there live many types of monkey: small monkeys of the macaque family, like the Rhesus monkey found in Afghanistan, northern India and southern China, or gibbon, which lives in southern Thailand, Singapore and Malaysia.

We also find big monkeys such as the orangutan, mainly in northern Singapore and in Malaysia. Its name means "old man of the woods" in Malaysian.

Tropical birds are also very common in the south and east of Asia. The great hornbill, a black and white bird, can be found in India, Thailand and Malaysia.

Many other types of animal live in India, like the Asian elephant, who has smaller ears than the African elephant, the Bengal tiger and many kinds of snake including the cobra.

Great Hornbill

Asian Elephant

Cobra

In Asia, as in other parts of the world, many species are threatened as their territories are destroyed by agriculture or deforestation, which is when people cut down trees for wood to make furniture or paper, for example. This is happening to the giant panda and the orangutan, who have less and less trees to feed themselves and to survive.

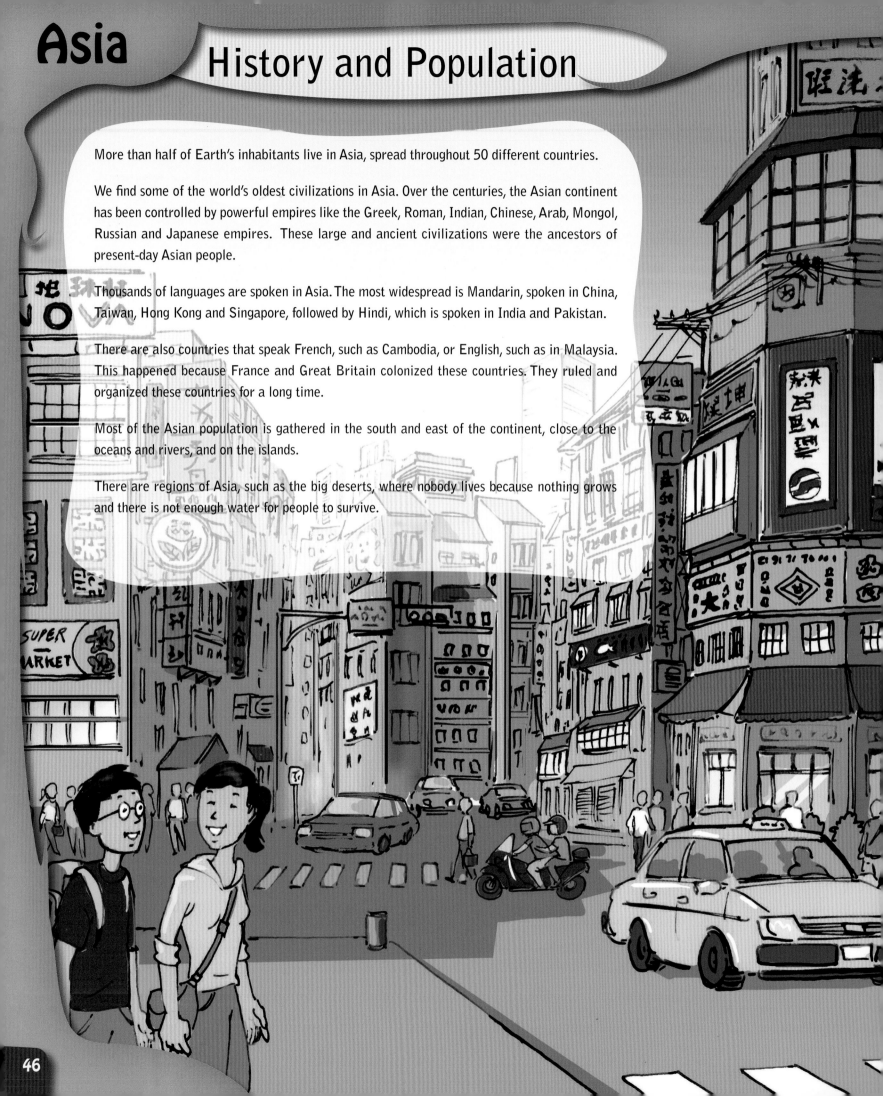

Asia

History and Population

More than half of Earth's inhabitants live in Asia, spread throughout 50 different countries.

We find some of the world's oldest civilizations in Asia. Over the centuries, the Asian continent has been controlled by powerful empires like the Greek, Roman, Indian, Chinese, Arab, Mongol, Russian and Japanese empires. These large and ancient civilizations were the ancestors of present-day Asian people.

Thousands of languages are spoken in Asia. The most widespread is Mandarin, spoken in China, Taiwan, Hong Kong and Singapore, followed by Hindi, which is spoken in India and Pakistan.

There are also countries that speak French, such as Cambodia, or English, such as in Malaysia. This happened because France and Great Britain colonized these countries. They ruled and organized these countries for a long time.

Most of the Asian population is gathered in the south and east of the continent, close to the oceans and rivers, and on the islands.

There are regions of Asia, such as the big deserts, where nobody lives because nothing grows and there is not enough water for people to survive.

Many Asians earn their living by cultivating tea and rice, their main source of food. These products are grown in the southern and eastern areas of the continent. The wealth of many Mideast countries comes from oil production.

Big cities like Tokyo, the most populated city in the world and the capital of Japan, have very advanced industries and therefore many factories.

The largest man-made structure in the world is the Great Wall of China, which is 4,160 miles (6,700 km) long. It crosses the country from the coast north of Beijing to the Gobi Desert.

War in places such as Iraq and Afghanistan, and natural disasters such as earthquakes and violent storms, make life difficult in many places in Asia.

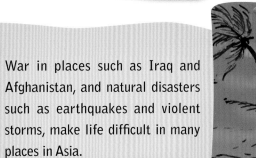

India has a very famous monument, the Taj Mahal, which means "Crown Palace." This monument is built out of white marble and situated on the Yamuna River, in the town of Agra.

Asia

Customs

There are many different countries and people in Asia and each have their own traditions and celebrations. The cuisine of Asia is also very diverse and recognized as some of the best in the world.

In China, the most important celebration is the Chinese New Year. As the Chinese people follow a lunar calendar, New Year's Day is not always celebrated on the same date.

Japan has many official celebrations. For example, the Flower Festival takes place every year on April 8. On this day, in temples thoughout the country, people celebrate the birth of Buddha, a saint who lived in Asia a very long time ago.

Buddha

In Japan, children must wear school uniforms. There are also no cafeterias in the schools; children have to take their meals with them. People often eat with chopsticks in Japan.

In Mongolia, people live in round tents known as yurts. It is a family dwelling with one room, which can easily be dismantled.

Thai people often greet each other with a "wai" to say hello: they join their hands together as if praying and bow gently.

In India, the cow is considered a sacred animal that represents peace. It is normal to see cows wandering freely around the towns and villages.

In Afghanistan, "Eid al-Fitr" is one of the biggest Islamic celebrations. On this day, Afghans celebrate the end of the month of Ramadan. During this period, people do not eat or drink during the daytime but only once at night. Most of the world's Muslims take part in Ramadan.

Maze

Dadmin the Mongol lost his horse while out on the steppes of Asia. Can you help him find his favorite steed?

→ Solution page 78

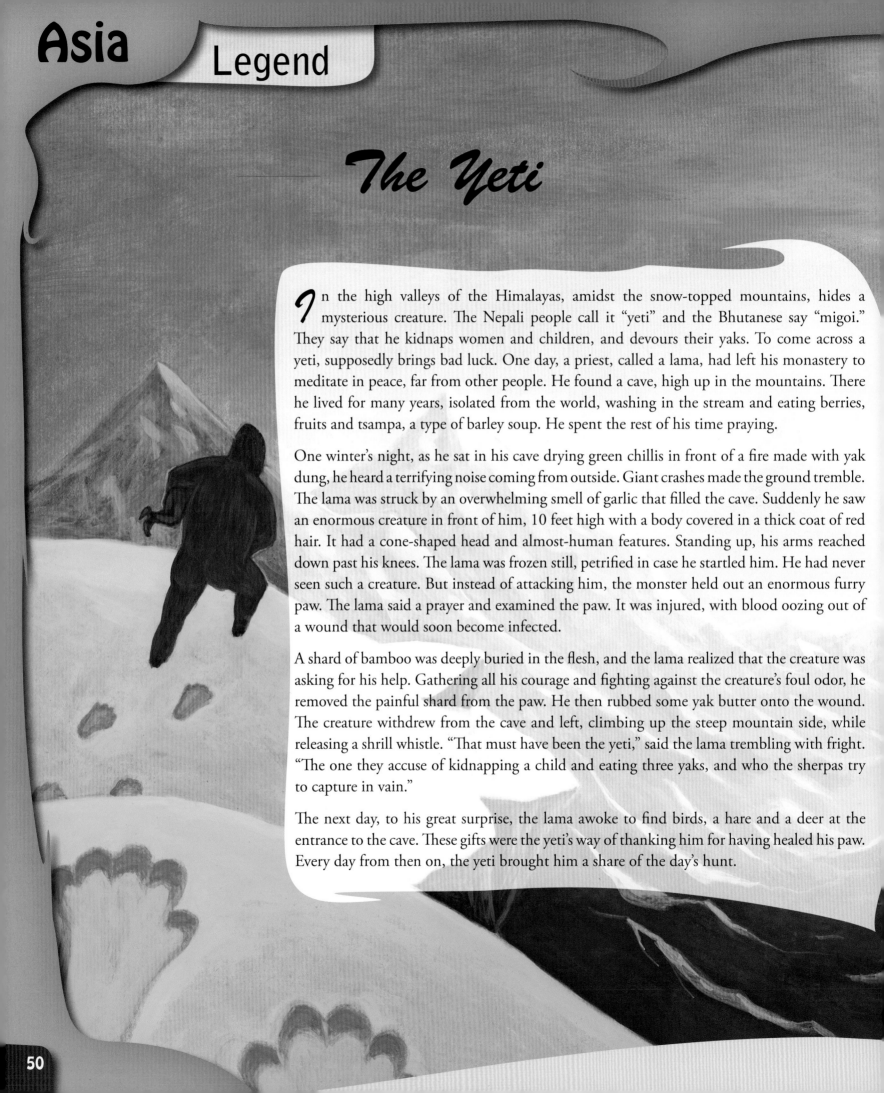

The Yeti

*I*n the high valleys of the Himalayas, amidst the snow-topped mountains, hides a mysterious creature. The Nepali people call it "yeti" and the Bhutanese say "migoi." They say that he kidnaps women and children, and devours their yaks. To come across a yeti, supposedly brings bad luck. One day, a priest, called a lama, had left his monastery to meditate in peace, far from other people. He found a cave, high up in the mountains. There he lived for many years, isolated from the world, washing in the stream and eating berries, fruits and tsampa, a type of barley soup. He spent the rest of his time praying.

One winter's night, as he sat in his cave drying green chillis in front of a fire made with yak dung, he heard a terrifying noise coming from outside. Giant crashes made the ground tremble. The lama was struck by an overwhelming smell of garlic that filled the cave. Suddenly he saw an enormous creature in front of him, 10 feet high with a body covered in a thick coat of red hair. It had a cone-shaped head and almost-human features. Standing up, his arms reached down past his knees. The lama was frozen still, petrified in case he startled him. He had never seen such a creature. But instead of attacking him, the monster held out an enormous furry paw. The lama said a prayer and examined the paw. It was injured, with blood oozing out of a wound that would soon become infected.

A shard of bamboo was deeply buried in the flesh, and the lama realized that the creature was asking for his help. Gathering all his courage and fighting against the creature's foul odor, he removed the painful shard from the paw. He then rubbed some yak butter onto the wound. The creature withdrew from the cave and left, climbing up the steep mountain side, while releasing a shrill whistle. "That must have been the yeti," said the lama trembling with fright. "The one they accuse of kidnapping a child and eating three yaks, and who the sherpas try to capture in vain."

The next day, to his great surprise, the lama awoke to find birds, a hare and a deer at the entrance to the cave. These gifts were the yeti's way of thanking him for having healed his paw. Every day from then on, the yeti brought him a share of the day's hunt.

This arrangement lasted a few years. One day, the lama awoke to find the entrance to the cave empty. He set off into the forest and followed the enormous footprints of the yeti across the snow. Close to a boulder, he found the hand and scalp of the yeti. He picked them up and returned down the mountain to the monastery. Once there, he told the other monks of this incredible adventure and showed them the hand and the scalp of the yeti. These strange remains of the "snow man" were displayed in the monastery, and many scientists studied them. Was the yeti a type of Asian monkey that had not been seen for years, a type of ground-living orangutan, or was it a Neanderthal man? No one knows, but those who have crossed his path will never forget him.

Europe

Europe stretches between the Arctic Ocean to the north and the Mediterranean Sea to the south. The western coast of Europe lies on the Atlantic Ocean, separating it from the United States. The Caspian Sea and the Ural Mountains separate Europe from Asia to the east.

ARCTIC OCEAN

NORTH CAPE

BARENTS SEA

ASIA

NORWEGIAN SEA

SCANDINAVIA

Lake Onega

Lake Ladoga

Ural mountains

ATLANTIC OCEAN

GULF OF BOTHNIA

BALTIC SEA

NORTH SEA

Thames R.

Rhine R.

Elbe R.

Vistula R.

ENGLISH CHANNEL

Seine R.

Loire R.

Garonne R.

Rhone R.

Po R.

Dnieper R.

Volga R.

Carpathian Mountains

Mount Elbrus (18,510 ft/5,642 m)

Ural Mountains

CASPIAN SEA

Ebro R.

Danube R.

BLACK SEA

Tagus R.

STRAIT OF GIBRALTAR

Europe lies entirely in the Northern Hemisphere.

MEDITERRANEAN SEA

ASIA

AFRICA

0   600 km
Scale

Map of Countries

Europe is the smallest continent after Oceania. It is one-quarter the size of Asia, but it is highly populated. More than one of out ten people on Earth live in Europe.

ARCTIC OCEAN

Novaya Zemlya (Russia)

Svalbard (Norway)

BARENTS SEA

ASIA

ICELAND
Reykjavik

NORWEGIAN SEA

RUSSIA

ATLANTIC OCEAN

NORTH SEA

SWEDEN
FINLAND
NORWAY
Oslo
Helsinki
Stockholm
Tallinn
ESTONIA
LATVIA
Riga
Moscow

BALTIC SEA

UNITED KINGDOM
Dublin
IRELAND
DENMARK
Copenhagen

LITHUANIA
Vilnius
Kaliningrad Oblast
Minsk
BELARUS

Amsterdam
GERMANY
London
NETHERLANDS
Brussels
Berlin
Warsaw
BELGIUM
POLAND
LUXEMBOURG
Paris
Prague
CZECH REPUBLIC
Kiev
UKRAINE

LIECHTENSTEIN
Vienna
SLOVAKIA
Bratislava
FRANCE
Bern
Vaduz
AUSTRIA
Budapest
MOLDOVA
SWITZERLAND
SLOVENIA
HUNGARY
ROMANIA
Zagreb
Ljubljana
CROATIA
Bucharest

CASPIAN SEA

PORTUGAL
ANDORRA
BOSNIA AND HERZEGOVINA
Belgrade
MONACO
Sarajevo
BLACK SEA
Madrid
ITALY
SERBIA AND MONTENEGRO
BULGARIA
Lisbon
Sofia
Rome
Skopje
SPAIN
Tirana
MACEDONIA
ALBANIA
Balearic Islands
GREECE

Europe is made up of 45 independent countries. Russia is the world's largest country, and Vatican City is the world's smallest.

MALTA
Valetta
Athens
CRETE

MEDITERRANEAN SEA
ASIA

AFRICA

0   600 km

Scale

53

Europe

Europe is composed of many different landscapes and geographical features. The mountain ranges of the north and south surround a large flat area in the center of the continent.

The oldest mountain ranges are in northern Europe. They are located in the United Kingdom (England, Northern Ireland, Scotland and Wales) and Scandinavia (Norway, Sweden, Denmark and Finland), the Massif Central and Vosges in France and the Black Forest in Germany.

The highest mountains are more recently formed and are found further south. They include the Pyrenees, the Alps, the Balkans, and the Caucasus.

The Pyrenees lie on the border of France and Spain. The Alps are at the crossroads of Switzerland, Austria, Italy and France. The Balkans are mainly in Bulgaria, and the Caucasus lie on the edge of Asia.

The highest summit in Europe is in the Caucasus Mountains. It is called Mount Elbrus, 18,51 feet (5,642 m) high.

Between these mountains are plains, vast open areas that are flat or with few hills. This land, which is fertile and therefore good to grow crops on, occupies most of the continent.

These plains and the extensive coastline of Europe makes it easy to move around and trade goods. There are many roads, railways, rivers, airports and shipping ports throughout Europe.

Climate

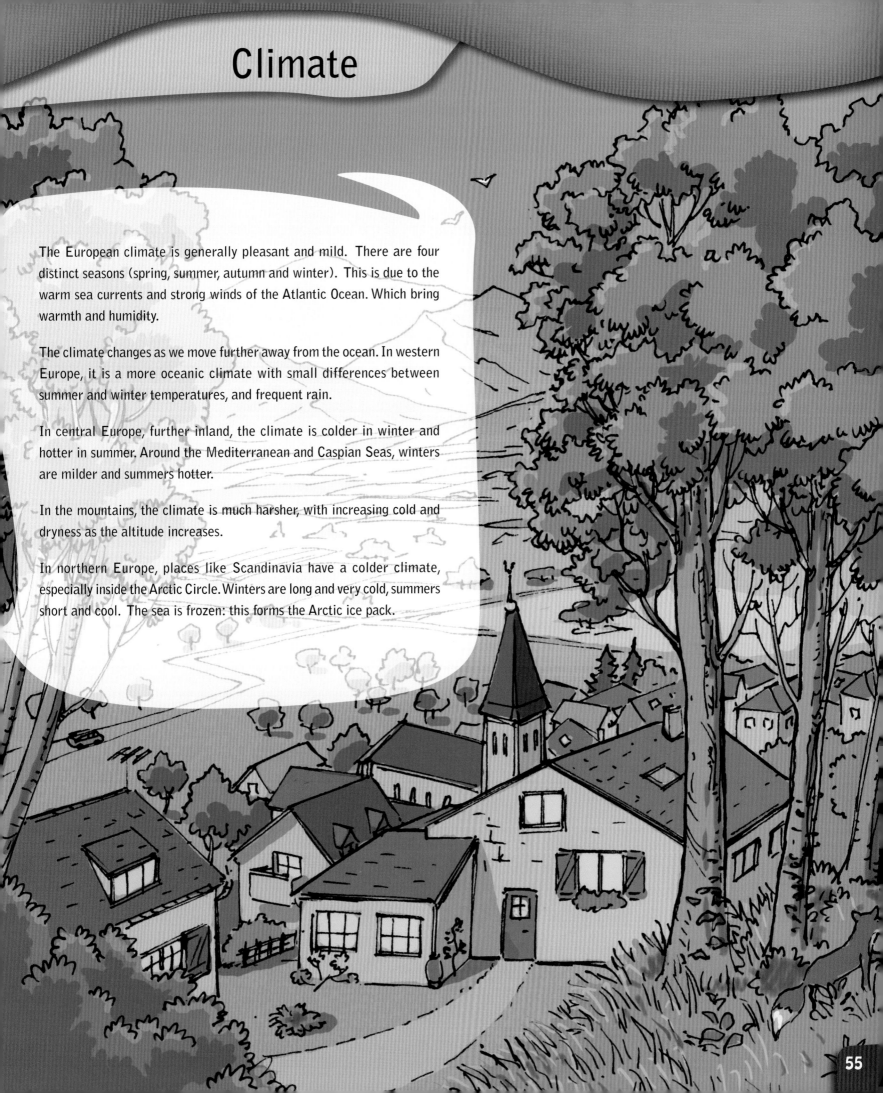

The European climate is generally pleasant and mild. There are four distinct seasons (spring, summer, autumn and winter). This is due to the warm sea currents and strong winds of the Atlantic Ocean. Which bring warmth and humidity.

The climate changes as we move further away from the ocean. In western Europe, it is a more oceanic climate with small differences between summer and winter temperatures, and frequent rain.

In central Europe, further inland, the climate is colder in winter and hotter in summer. Around the Mediterranean and Caspian Seas, winters are milder and summers hotter.

In the mountains, the climate is much harsher, with increasing cold and dryness as the altitude increases.

In northern Europe, places like Scandinavia have a colder climate, especially inside the Arctic Circle. Winters are long and very cold, summers short and cool. The sea is frozen: this forms the Arctic ice pack.

Europe

Plants

The landscapes of Europe are very varied, depending on the differences in terrain and climate. Fields, mountains and forests still occupy a lot of space away from the big cities.

Most of Europe consists of plains covered in cultivated fields and forests. We find two main types of forest on the European continent: deciduous forests and boreal forests.

The temperate deciduous forests are common in central and southern Europe. They are made up of trees that lose their leaves in the winter.

Europe's vegetation is rapidly giving way to growing cities, factories and businesses. Many organizations, however, are working to preserve Europe's plant life and natural beauty.

The boreal forest, closer to the North Pole, is made up of evergreen conifers, such as the pine tree, which do not lose their needles in the winter.

Animals

Otter

Europe was once almost entirely covered in forest. Today, there is much less as they have been removed to make space for towns and cities. Some animals that were once common, such as otters, are becoming more rare.

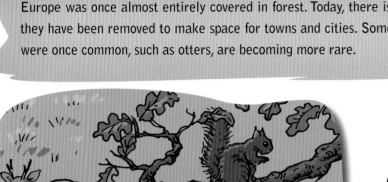

Mouflon

Chamois

Some animals have adapted to their changing environments, including foxes, weasels, badgers, squirrels, owls and various types of deer.

Ibex

In the mountains, we find the chamois, the mouflon and, more rarely, the ibex.

Elk

In the north, we find moose, brown bears, ground squirrels and wood grouse.

Lynx

A small number of lynx have survived in the forests of southern Europe.

Many birds, such as eagles, storks, horned owls and swallows, spend the summer in the north. They migrate to warmer regions in the winter.

Europe

Most European countries share a common history. They were heavily influenced by the ancient Greeks and Romans. The Greek alphabet and Roman letters led to the development of writing in Europe.

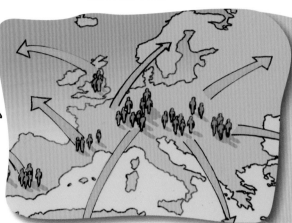

Europe has had a worldwide influence because its explorers and merchants traveled and spread their ideas for many centuries.

The country borders in Europe have changed many times over the centuries, due to wars, agreements and royal marriages.

After World War I and World War II (1914-1918 and 1939-1945), the Europeans decided to unite and help bring peace. At the end of World War II, in 1945, Europe was divided into two blocs: Western Europe, which included the more developed countries and was allied with the United States, and Eastern Europe, controlled by the USSR (Union of Soviet Socialist Republics). The continent was symbolically divided by the Berlin Wall, in eastern Germany.

In 1989, the Berlin Wall was taken down. Germany was reunited and the Soviet Union collapsed. The former Soviet states gradually returned to free rule. A new Europe was born.

Over recent years, many countries have joined the European Union, found in 1992 by 12 countries to defend their freedom and protect human rights. Today, the European Union includes 27 countries.

Hundreds of languages are spoken in Europe. The most common is German, spoken in Germany, Austria, Switzerland and Luxembourg. English, French, Spanish and Italian are the other common languages.

French is the only official language in France. Some regional languages are still spoken and taught, however, including Breton (in Brittany) and Basque (southern France).

Population

The most highly populated European countries are Germany, France, the United Kingdom, Italy and Spain. Germany has the highest population, but France and Ireland have the most number of births per person.

Europe features many different forms of economic activity. In some countries, such as Poland, France, the Ukraine and Belgium, agriculture is the main activity.

Europe is one of the richest continents, but the wealth is spread unevenly. The gap between the richer countries of Western and northern Europe, and the Eastern European countries that once lived under USSR control, is large.

Some economies, as in England, Switzerland and Luxembourg, thrive because of their banking industries. The economies of Italy and Germany are aided by their car manufacturing, and Norway and England are large producers of oil and gas.

The European Union aims to encourage trade between the Union's different countries with the tax-free circulation of products and the use of a single currency called the Euro.

Parthenon

London Bridge

Colosseum

Kremlin

Eiffel Tower

Europe is the most popular tourist destination for people from around the world. The most famous monuments are the Eiffel Tower in Paris, the Colosseum in Rome, the Tower of London and its famous bridge, the Parthenon in Athens and the Kremlin in Moscow.

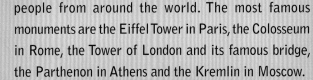

Europe

The people of Europe have different customs and festivities depending on their origins. Today, daily life is very similar everywhere, but local customs are proudly retained.

European cuisine is very varied. There are many regional specialties, including fish and chips in England, paella in Spain, goulash in Hungary and nettle soup in Ireland.

There are many celebrations throughout the year. Some exist only in certain regions while others take place in many countries. Saint Nicolas, who brings candy and gifts to children on the nights of December 5th and 6th, or Christmas, is honored throughout Europe.

Carnivals are also a big part of European celebrations. There is the carnival of Binche in Belgium, the Venice carnival in Italy and one in Nice, France.

Not all European countries follow the same daily schedule. In the north, people eat dinner at about 6 P.M. But in the south, as in Spain, they eat at about 10 P.M., and shops close later. German, Finnish and Danish schoolchildren have academic lessons only in the morning. Afternoons are dedicated to sports and art.

People have different manners from one country to another. For example, whereas most people say "yes" by nodding their head, this means "no" to a Bulgarian. In Holland, people congratulate the family of the person whose birthday it is. In Germany, it is impolite to wrap flowers.

"That's not Catalina, it's my nurse's daughter!"

The imposter Catalina said :
"Don't you recognize me?"
The king was furious and cried at Bernardo:
"You lied to me, and you will go to prison for this, but I will keep my word and marry your sister."
They were married joylessly.

One day, Catalina asked if she could leave the whale's stomach and breath some fresh air.
The whale agreed, but attached her with a golden chain so that she would not be able to escape.
Catalina climbed out and went to sit next to a spring. As she brushed her hair, pearls fell from her
comb. A fisherman watched her. A dove came and sat on her shoulder.
"If only I could fly like you, I would know what has happened to my brother and my fiancé!"

"Your brother is in prison and your fiancé married the daughter of your nurse," replied the dove.
Catalina cried and the rain began to fall.
"Don't cry," said the dove. "Seven days from now, I will bring you news."

Catalina smiled and the sun returned. The dove flew away and the young lady went back inside the
whale's stomach. On the shore, the fisherman went to the village and told the people everything
he had seen. Soon, everybody was talking about the beautiful girl of the sea. Even the king heard
the story and remembered the words of Bernardo:
"When she brushes her hair, pearls fall from her comb." He went to the shore himself. After
eight days, Catalina emerged from the sea. The king had never seen such a beautiful girl!
She sat close to the shore, untied her hair and pearls fell from her comb. A dove came and sat on
her shoulder:

"What news do you have?" asked Catalina.
"Your brother is in prison and the king is still married to your nurse's daughter!"
Catalina began to cry and the rain began to fall. The king came out of his hiding place, cut
the chain and told her:
"I am your fiancé, the king of Spain, and I have come for you."
Catalina smiled and the sun began to shine. The king released Bernardo from prison, banished
the nurse and her daughter, and married the beautiful Catalina who makes the rain fall when
she cries and the sun shine when she smiles. Since that day, the sun shines in Spain.

Oceania

The Land

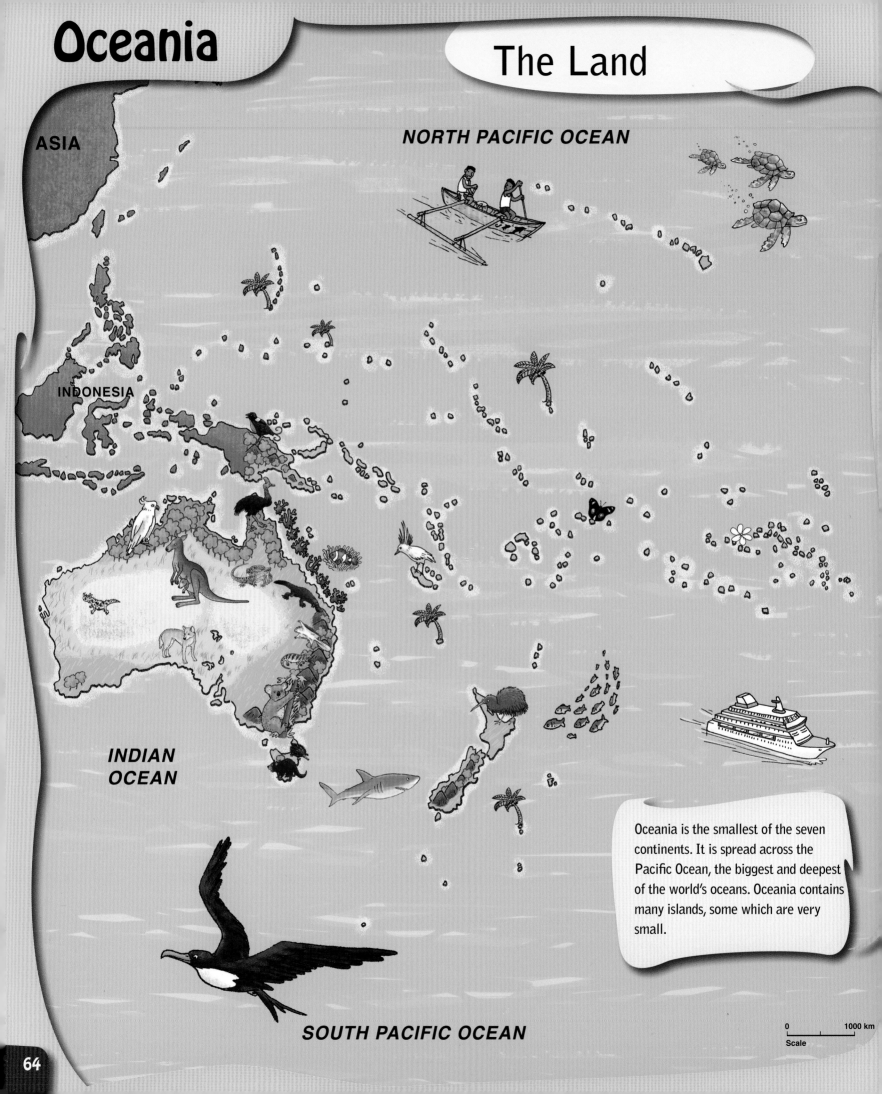

ASIA

NORTH PACIFIC OCEAN

INDONESIA

INDIAN OCEAN

SOUTH PACIFIC OCEAN

Oceania is the smallest of the seven continents. It is spread across the Pacific Ocean, the biggest and deepest of the world's oceans. Oceania contains many islands, some which are very small.

0   1000 km
Scale

Map of Countries

Australia is Oceania's largest island, but it is not very heavily populated. Most people live on the coast. There are large desert regions in the center of the country.

NORTH PACIFIC OCEAN

Honolulu

HAWAII

MARSHALL ISLANDS

NORTHERN MARIANA ISLANDS

PALAU

FEDERATED STATES OF MICRONESIA

INDONESIA

PAPUA NEW GUINEA

NAURU

KIRIBATI

SOLOMON ISLANDS

TUVALU

TOKELAU

SAMOA

AMERICAN SAMOA

WALLIS AND FUTUNA

COOK ISLANDS

CORAL SEA ISLANDS TERRITORY

VANUATU

NEW CALEDONIA

Noumea

TONGA

FIJI ISLANDS

Papeete

FRENCH POLYNESIA

PITCAIRN ISLANDS

AUSTRALIA

Canberra

Sydney

Melbourne

Auckland

TASMAN SEA

TASMANIA

Wellington

NEW ZEALAND

INDIAN OCEAN

Papua New Guinea is Oceania's second largest country. The third largest, New Zealand, is made up of two main islands and a few smaller ones. Most people live in North Island, a less mountainous region.

SOUTH PACIFIC OCEAN

The region known as Polynesia includes islands in the central and south Pacific. Melanesia is the region north and northeast of Australia. Micronesia includes islands in the western Pacific. Each region features many different languages, customs and religions.

0   1000 km

Scale

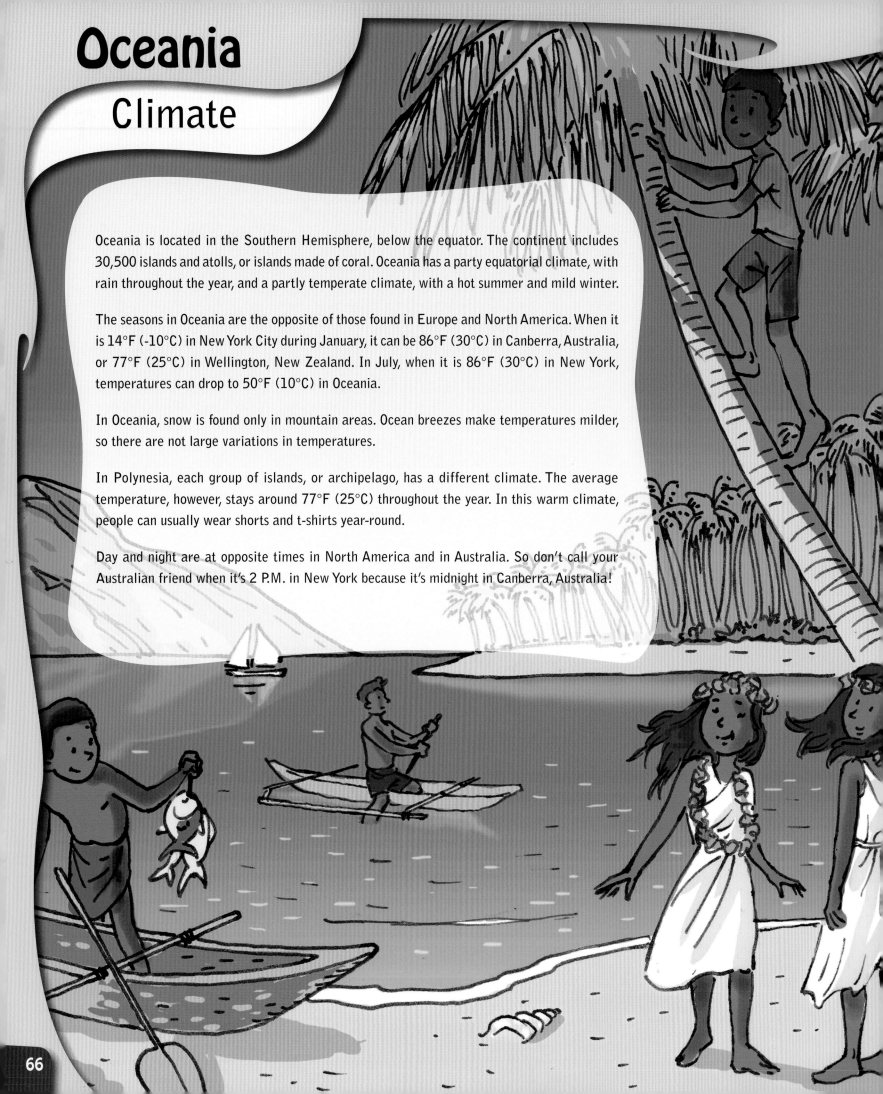

Oceania
Climate

Oceania is located in the Southern Hemisphere, below the equator. The continent includes 30,500 islands and atolls, or islands made of coral. Oceania has a party equatorial climate, with rain throughout the year, and a partly temperate climate, with a hot summer and mild winter.

The seasons in Oceania are the opposite of those found in Europe and North America. When it is 14°F (-10°C) in New York City during January, it can be 86°F (30°C) in Canberra, Australia, or 77°F (25°C) in Wellington, New Zealand. In July, when it is 86°F (30°C) in New York, temperatures can drop to 50°F (10°C) in Oceania.

In Oceania, snow is found only in mountain areas. Ocean breezes make temperatures milder, so there are not large variations in temperatures.

In Polynesia, each group of islands, or archipelago, has a different climate. The average temperature, however, stays around 77°F (25°C) throughout the year. In this warm climate, people can usually wear shorts and t-shirts year-round.

Day and night are at opposite times in North America and in Australia. So don't call your Australian friend when it's 2 P.M. in New York because it's midnight in Canberra, Australia!

Plants

There are thick forests and many grasslands throughout Oceania. Plant life is abundant except in central Australia, which is covered in a large desert of red earth. In Australia, people live mainly on the coast because the climate there is milder and the inhabitants have easier access to water.

Animals

Tasmanian Devil

In Australia and Tasmania, there are many animals that are found nowhere else in the world: the kangaroo, possum, koala bear, platypus and tasmanian devil.

In New Zealand, we find many types of birds, including the kiwi, which cannot fly, and the kakapo, a large parrot. The tuatara is a type of lizard that lives only in New Zealand.

Kakapo

Spotted Cuscus

Birds in New Guinea include the flightless cassowary and the bird-of-paradise. The spotted cuscus is a furry relative of the koala bear.

Lory

On the Pacific Islands, there are many very colorful birds, like the lory or the crowned pigeon. The kagu is an animal that lives only in New Caledonia.

Oceania

History and Population

Oceania is the least populated region in the world. The inhabitants of Oceania are mainly descendants of people who arrived from Asia thousands of years ago or people who came from Europe more recently.

Today, Australia and New Zealand still have close ties with Great Britain. Before the English arrived in these areas, only the Aborigines, a people originally from Asia, lived in Australia. New Zealand was originally the home of the Maoris, from Polynesia.

Some islands in Oceania are part of other countries. New Caledonia and French Polynesia belong to France. Hawaii is part of the United States.

The official language in Australia and New Zealand is English because these regions were colonized by Great Britain.

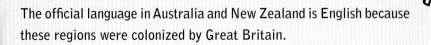

The island of New Guinea is divided into two countries, each in a different continent. Indonesia is in Asia, and Papua New Guinea is in Oceania. Although the official language is English, more than 700 languages are spoken in these places.

The Papuan people of New Guinea, a tribal people, lived like in ancient times Until recently, the Papuan people of New Guinea, a tribal people, lived as they did in ancient times, because they had never met people outside their own tribe. It took the Europeans a long time to visit the mountainous and isolated regions in the center of the countries.

Polynesians and Micronesians live mainly by farming, especially coconuts, and tourism.

Each year, millions of visitors from around the world come to the islands of Oceania to enjoy the landscape, climate and cultures of the region.

Oceania

National holidays and customs in Oceania are very similar to those found in Europe. In Australia, New Zealand and Polynesia, people celebrate Christmas, Easter and other important religious Christian dates. Christmas festivities are often celebrated on the beach.

Among the ancient tribes of Polynesia, Melanesia and Micronesia, we find many different customs and cultural practices. These have been passed from generation to generation through a rich tradition of storytelling.

Before the Europeans arrived in Oceania, native parents told stories or sung songs to their children, which included myths and the tales about the origins of mankind. To this day, it is difficult to write some of the Polynesian languages such as Maori. The languages were originally meant to be spoken, not written.

Boats are the main form of travel in Oceania. There is almost one boat for every inhabitant of the region. They include small fishing boats to large ferries, which travel between the islands.

Throughout the islands, the rich and diverse artwork of the many different tribes is also transmitted from one generation to the next. The Papuan people of New Guinea wear mother of pearl jewelry, paint their faces and create elaborate hairstyles to impress each other.

1 I am the country where the kangaroo lives. Who am I?

2

These people live in Papua New Guinea. Who are they? Rearrange the following letters for the correct answer: **APUPNA**

3 What is the capital city of New Zealand ?
a) Christchurch
b) Auckland
c) Wellington

4

I am a large bird that lives in New Guinea and does not fly. What am I?
a) a kiwi
b) a cassowary
c) a tuatara

5 I am part of France. Who am I?
a) Australia
b) Tasmania
c) New Caledonia

→ Solutions page 78

Legend

The Rainbow Snake

A long time ago, there was the dreamtime, before the men, plants and animals existed. The earth was flat, immobile and plunged into darkness. The rainbow snake slept deeply, buried in the center of the earth. One day, he woke with a start and broke out through the earth's crust, leaving a trail of red ochre dust behind him. Slithering along the ground, his long body created the mountain ranges and dug out the abrupt canyons and deep valleys.

He then decided it was time to create light and life. The sun shone in the sky and lit up the world, while the moon took its place below the stars. The snake was so powerful that a violent rain fell from the sky, filling the canyons and filling the valleys that his body had dug out during his journey. The lakes, rivers and seas were created. The places where the snake had not gone became flat deserts. Then the snake began to name all the creatures who lived in the center of the earth and asked them to go and live on the surface. So he named the animals: parrot, bat, emu, echidna, frilled lizard, koala bear, kangaroo, wallaby, platypus…

And then came the first humans, the Aborigines. The snake said to them:

"This is your country, you must never leave it. Live at peace with the animals, respect the trees, the rocks and the earth, as every creation has its own spirit. Pass this knowledge on to your children, and be the guardians of this land."

One day, the snake passed through a desert in the center of Australia. The air was so hot and the earth so dry that no man, plant or animal could survive there.

The snake thought about it and decided to plant a giant grain in the middle of the desert.

He thought that a giant tree would grow from the grain, covering the plain with its foliage and protecting the earth with its shade. Once protected from the sun's scorching rays, the earth would become fertile. Trees and flowers would grow again, and kangaroos, wallabies and possums would come to live there. "It will be a perfect dreamland," thought the snake, pleased with his idea. Like magic, a giant grain appeared in the middle of the desert. The snake asked the sky to make the rain fall heavily. Unfortunately, the grain was too big and it could never rain enough to make it sprout. With time, the grain became hard and transformed into a giant block of sandstone: "Uluru," the sacred rock of the Aborigine people. When the scarce rains fall on Uluru, the red rock becomes a silver grey color. Frogs appear and life all around appears to hold its breath, waiting for the miraculous burst of life that they have been expecting for so long. The Anangu people say that the rainbow snake, who controls water, the source of life, still sleeps in one of the rock pools on top of Uluru.

Antarctica

Antarctica, which contains the South Pole, is the seventh continent on Earth. It is the coldest region on our planet. Temperatures can drop to -128°F (-89°C). About 98 percent of Antarctica is covered by ice, which averages at least 1 mile (1.6 km) in thickness.

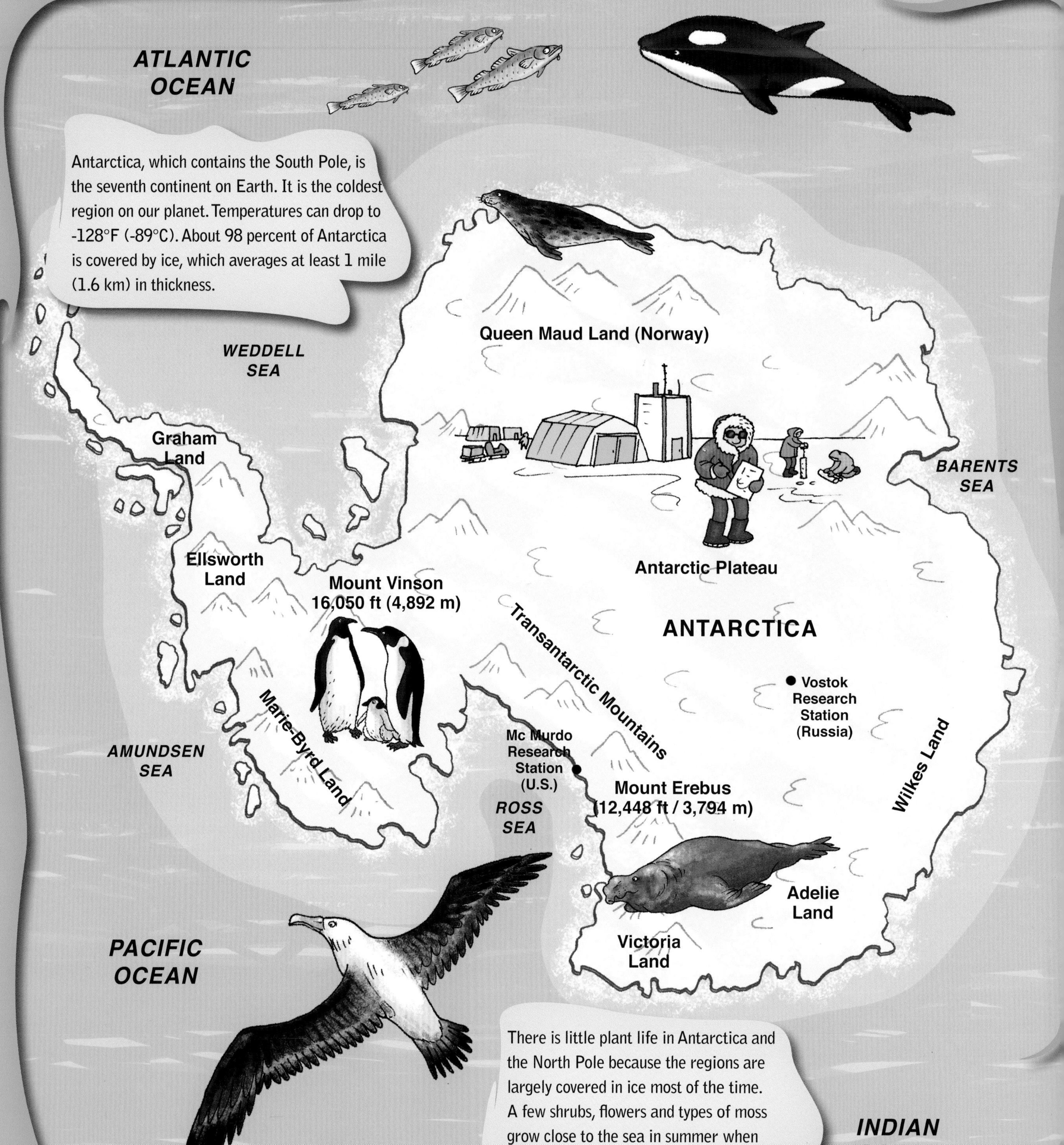

WEDDELL
SEA

Queen Maud Land (Norway)

Graham
Land

BARENTS
SEA

Ellsworth
Land

Mount Vinson
16,050 ft (4,892 m)

Antarctic Plateau

ANTARCTICA

Transantarctic Mountains

• Vostok
Research
Station
(Russia)

Marie-Byrd Land

Wilkes Land

AMUNDSEN
SEA

Mc Murdo
Research
Station
(U.S.)

ROSS
SEA

Mount Erebus
(12,448 ft / 3,794 m)

Adelie
Land

PACIFIC
OCEAN

Victoria
Land

There is little plant life in Antarctica and the North Pole because the regions are largely covered in ice most of the time. A few shrubs, flowers and types of moss grow close to the sea in summer when the ice melts.

INDIAN
OCEAN

The North Pole

BERING STRAIT

Alaska
(United States)

CHUKCHI SEA

RUSSIA

CANADA

BEAUFORT
SEA

EAST SIBERIAN
SEA

LAPTEV
SEA

ARCTIC OCEAN

Ellesmere Island

Qaanaaq

BAFFIN BAY

SPITZBERG
(Norway)

GREENLAND
(Denmark)

The North Pole is in the middle
of the Arctic Ocean, not on land.
The South Pole is on
the continent of Antarctica.

BARENTS
SEA

NORTH
CAPE

Nuuk

NORWAY
SEA

The North Pole includes the
northernmost regions of Europe,
Asia and North America. The ice
sheets of the region stretch as
far as Greenland.

Reykjavik

ATLANTIC
OCEAN

ICELAND

The Poles

Climate

At the North Pole, the sun sets in September and is not seen for the next six months of winter. In March, it rises and does not set during the summer months. The weather is very cold in winter, with temperatures below zero. In summer, it is warmer but still around zero.

The seasons at the South Pole are the opposite of those at the North Pole. When it is winter and always dark at the North Pole, it is summer and daytime at the South Pole.

The climate is harsher at the South Pole because it is very cold and there are strong winds throughout the year. Temperatures are always below zero.

Animals

Snowy Owl

Walrus

Caribou

Arctic Hare

At the North Pole, we find thick-furred animals such as the polar bear, arctic hare, arctic fox and birds such as the snowy owl. Caribou, seals and walruses also live in this region of the world.

At the South Pole, there are very few animals. We find sea birds, including penguins, petrels and fulmars as well as seals and elephant seals.

The oceans around both poles are full of many different fish and whales.

History and Population

The North Pole is home to the Sami people of Scandinavia, the Inuits of Canada, Alaska and Greenland, and the Samoyedic people of Siberia. All came from Asia, except the Inuits, who were already living in North America in prehistoric times.

Scientists are the only people who live in Antarctica. They have come to study polar life. The continent does not belong to any country. Instead, nations have agreed that only scientists can live there.

Customs

The people of the Poles fish and hunt, mainly seals. They make clothes and mattresses from the seal skin and make lamps with seal fat. Some people raise caribou or reindeer.

Around the North Pole, people live in stone and wooden huts. Igloos are built for shelter during storms and overnight stays during the fishing season.

Ecology

For centuries, people have abused nature by harming wildlife, forests and the atmosphere. Many types of plants and animals are now extinct, or no longer living.

In the North and South polar regions, the ice sheets are melting, causing icebergs to break off and float in the sea. These are enormous chunks of frozen freshwater. The rising temperature of Earth's atmosphere and oceans are causing the ice sheets in the polar regions to melt. Enormous icebergs of frozen freshwater break off and float in the sea. This global warming causes us to lose these valuable freshwater resources as they melt away into the ocean.

Today, people are showing increased care for the earth. Our goal is to live more in harmony with nature while being able to meet the needs of all people. Hopefully, we will leave our planet clean and bountiful for future generations around the world.

Puzzle solutions

P. 17 Africa

Quick Quiz:

1) A volcano
2) The Sahara
3) Henna
4) In the African forests
5) Savanna
6) Baobab tree
7) Lion
8) A *djellaba*
9) A lake
10) Lemur

P. 27 North America

Maze: Nagawiki lives in a teepee.

P. 37 South America

Riddles:

1) My first part is the first letter of the compass point opposite of south, my second is another word for me, my third part is a popular type of transport, my fourth part is the spanish word for water and my whole is NICARAGUA.

2) My first part is what I eat my breakfast cereal from, minus W, my second part is the letter that follows H in the alphabet, my third part means to go by somewhere and my whole is BOLIVIA.

3) Argentina
4) A gaucho
5) Brasilia

P. 49 Asia

Maze: Did you find Dadmin's horse?

P. 61 Europe

Name that Sea!:

1) **M**adrid
2) **E**lbrus
3) **D**enmark
4) **I**taly
5) **T**ower (Eiffel Tower)
6) **E**lbe
7) **R**ussia
8) **R**omania
9) **A**thens
10) **N**orway
11) **E**uro
12) **A**ustria
13) **N**orth Sea

| M | E | D | I | T | E | R | R | A | N | E | A | N |

P. 71 Oceania

Quick Quiz:

1) Australia
2) Papuan
3) (c) Wellington
4) (b) The cassowary
5) (c) New Caledonia

Index

Index